WHITMAN AND NIETZSCHE

UNIVERSITY OF NORTH CAROLINA
STUDIES IN THE GERMANIC LANGUAGES
AND LITERATURES

Publication Committee

FREDERIC E. COENEN, EDITOR

WERNER P. FRIEDERICH   GEORGE S. LANE

JOHN G. KUNSTMANN   HERBERT W. REICHERT

For other volumes in this series see page 232.

Foreign Sales through:
Librairie E. Droz
8 Rue Verdaine
Geneva, Switzerland

NUMBER FORTY-EIGHT

UNIVERSITY
OF NORTH CAROLINA
STUDIES IN
THE GERMANIC LANGUAGES
AND LITERATURES

WHITMAN AND NIETZSCHE

A COMPARATIVE STUDY OF
THEIR THOUGHT

by *Constantine*
C. N. STAVROU

CHAPEL HILL
THE UNIVERSITY OF NORTH CAROLINA PRESS
1964

Printed in the Netherlands by Royal VanGorcum Ltd., Assen

Go, dear friend, if need be give up all else, and commence
to-day to inure yourself to pluck, reality, self-esteem,
definiteness, elevatedness,
Rest not till you rivet and publish yourself of your own
Personality.

WHITMAN

What dost thou Believe in? – In this: That the weights of
all things must be determined anew.

NIETZSCHE

My final merit I refuse you –
I refuse putting from me what I really am;
Encompass worlds, but never try to encompass me.

WHITMAN

My opinion is *my* opinion: another person has not easily a
right to it.

NIETZSCHE

VII

CONTENTS

All pagination, unless otherwise indicated, will refer to the following texts. Quotations from *Leaves of Grass*, the *Prefaces* (to the various editions of *Leaves of Grass*), and *Democratic Vistas* are from the 1891-92 ("deathbed edition") compiled by James E. Miller Jr. (Riverside Edition, Houghton Mifflin, 1959). Quotations from *Specimen Days* are from the text edited by Richard Chase (Signet Classic, CP-104, The New American Library, New York, 1961). Quotations from *Twilight of The Idols, The Will to Power*, and *The Antichrist* are from the translation by Walter Kaufmann (*The Portable Nietzsche*, The Viking Press, 1954). Quotations from *Joyful Wisdom* are from the translation by Kurt F. Reinhardt (Atlantic Paperbacks, Frederick Unger Publishing Company, 1960). Quotations from *The Birth of Tragedy* and *The Genealogy of Morals* are from the translation of Francis Golffing (A Doubleday Anchor Book, A81, Doubleday & Company, 1956). Quotations from *Beyond Good And Evil* are from the translation by Marianne Cowan (Gateway Edition, Henry Regnery Company, 1955). Quotations from *Thus Spoke Zarathustra* (indicated *Zarathustra*) are from *The Portable Nietzsche* or from the translation by R. J. Hollingdale (Penguin Books, L-118, Great Britain, 1961). All quotations from *Ecce Homo* are from *The Philosophy of Nietzsche* (*Modern Library*, New York, 1927). All quotations of Nietzsche by Albert Camus are taken from *The Rebel* (Translated by Anthony Bower, Vintage Books, K-30, New York, 1957).

TO THE MEMORY OF MY MOTHER

EUPHEMIA STAVROU

January 22, 1892 - March 26, 1964

A writer's ideas are often better understood when considered side by side with those of another. This is especially true when both are of the same intellectual milieu, and their works overflow with innumerable parallelisms. Frequently, a thought which may sound jejune in one will sound singularly penetrating and unique in the other. Sometimes what is obscure or ambiguous in the first writer's verbiage may emerge as an original insight in the phrasing of the second writer. One writer may detail his thought processes and thus aid the reader who experiences difficulty ciphering the other's logic of the intuitive heart. On occasion, a doctrine regarded as subsidiary in the canon of one writer may mark the precise point of divarication between his thinking and that of the second writer, and may therefore indicate a need for further inquiry. In addition, borrowings as well as demarcations from acknowledged common sources afford dependable calipers with which to gauge the originality of each of two borrowers.

A comparative study of two authors' works makes it possible to become thoroughly, if not authoritatively, familiar with their philosophy. No study-in-depth of an individual author is more exacting and informative than the labor entailed by the comparative approach. Constant rereading, cross-checking, and collating of similarities in the writings of two men is often the means of developing the student into scholar. The comparative approach, moreover, is excellent pedagogy. Nothing serves as well as analogy when one seeks to enforce and clarify a particularly troublesome facet of a writer's thinking. But perhaps the greatest advantage of a comparative study is the mental stimulation it generates. As the detection of one illuminating similarity follows fast upon another, one feels an excitement akin to the pleasurable anticipation of the explorer or inventor. And this holds doubly true when the subjects of a study are as dynamic, challenging, appealing, and mesmerizing as Walt Whitman and Friedrich Nietzsche.

The present essay does not aim at completeness, still less at finality. It undertakes only to clarify the extent and nature of the similarity in the thought of Whitman and Nietzsche and to assemble parallel texts toward this end. So far as is known, there is no evidence which claims Walt Whitman (1819-1892) directly influenced the thought of Friedrich Nietzsche (1844-1900). Since Whitman had virtually finished his life and life's work before Nietzsche had hardly commenced his, it is within the realm of possibility that the precocious Nietzsche, who admired Emerson though he detested Carlyle, had read the perfervid disciple of the Great Brahmin. But nothing can be produced to support this intriguing speculation. No direct link between the two exists. Although both Whitman and Nietzsche freely admit their respective debts to Emerson, Nietzsche never mentions or alludes to Whitman.

The affinities between the two, however, are not only unmistakable but remarkably extensive. In countless ways, the work of the one inevitably puts

2

one in mind of the work of the other. One can readily discover many instances where the mode and manner of their expression are very much the same. Identical arguments are used by both to argue for or against a particular doctrine. The similarities in their intuitive and psychological apperceptions, in fact, are so astonishing – from many inconsequent and minor peculiarities and idiosyncrasies of statement to very minute details of their ideas – that even the respects in which they differ make their common features all the more striking. Nor can this resemblance be cavalierly dismissed or discounted by saying that, actually, it consists of little more than the inevitable likenesses discoverable in all iconoclasts who spurn convention. After all, countless others, equally endowed and equally articulate, were born into, and inveighed against, the intellectual climate to which Whitman and Nietzsche were exposed. But none of these resemble Whitman and Nietzsche as much as Whitman and Nietzsche resemble each other. Where their ideas are most alike, we are invariably reminded of William Blake and D. H. Lawrence. Yet, even the latter are closer to each other than either is to Whitman or Nietzsche. Nietzsche's thought echoes Whitman's in a sufficient number of important particulars to command the serious attention of both teachers and students.

In the history of mankind, great discoveries and the well-nigh identical formulation of them have been known to occur simultaneously in widely-separated regions of the globe. They occur in all

3

areas of human endeavor. Whitman and Nietzsche might be an instance of such an occurrence. Be that as it may, we must be mindful that it is the fact of the occurrence, and not its cause, which concerns us here. It is by a careful examination of this occurrence that I hope to show that Whitman's stature as a thinker and psychologist has not been accorded the recognition of which it is so richly deserving. That no one has deemed it worthwhile to pursue at any length the large extent to which Nietzsche's thought runs parallel to Whitman's, tacitly oppugns the still-proliferating plethora of biographical, as opposed to critical, Whitmaniana. Despite the commendable pioneering work of Frederik Schyberg (*Walt Whitman*, translated from the Danish by E. A. Allen. New York, 1951) and Roger Asselineau (*The Evolution of Walt Whitman: The Creation of a Personality*. Cambridge, 1960), the comprehension and appreciation of the thought in *Leaves of Grass* remain sadly inadequate. Although Mody Boatright studied Whitman's debt to Hegel in the 1920's, and, although, more recently, James E. Miller, Jr. has competently undertaken to demonstrate that Whitman was a more systematic and profound thinker than he is generally acknowledged to have been, the Whitman sceptics and disparagers are still among us in disproportionately large numbers. In the academician's proverbial rationalization for ingurgitation or dilettantism, a great deal still demands and has to be done.

This monograph aspires to be a modest contribution to the increasing number of studies which

4

valiantly, albeit not always successfully, have sought to present Whitman less as a superior Vachel Lindsay and more as a slightly inferior William Blake or William Butler Yeats. By investigating the similitude in the thinking of Whitman and Nietzsche, it hopes to discourage the disrating of Whitman through condescending or tolerantly-amused commentaries. Whitman is so deceptively simple, so admittedly awkward in his banalities, so professedly prolix, so extravagant and eccentric of utterance, so unabashedly frank and forthright, so disconcertingly earthy, so terrifyingly honest, so unnaturally and inhumanly free of hypocrisy, ulterior motivation, and literary pretension, that inane misinterpretations, which see him as a tedious chauvinist, or a mindless optimist, or a blathering exhibitionist, or a depraved eroticist, or a befuddled invert, continue to pour out of publishing houses and to be sensationally reviewed by *Time*. It is very like the misapprehension which, for a long time, and naturally with a different animus and direction, plagued Nietzsche. And, even today, despite generous tributes by litterateurs such as Shaw, Mann, Sartre, and Camus, as well as virtual apotheosis by the existentialists, every so often, one comes across abusive attacks against Nietzsche as a Socratic empoisoner of youth, and as the embodiment of the worst of Borgia, Machiavelli, Spengler, and Hitler. But, whereas, in the last decade, leastways, Nietzsche has been indeed fortunate in having such capable and brilliant expounders and apologists as Kazan-

5

tzakis in Greece, Camus in France, H. J. Blackham in England, and Kaufmann of Princeton and Reinhardt of Stanford in America, Whitman has not fared half as well. Now, as ever, Whitman is cursed with a surfeit of youthful Henry Jameses. Altogether too often, Whitman, like a hapless Gulliver, has been metaphorically staked to the ground by petty Lilliputians who have prodded indefatigably and indelicately with distorted perspectives, unedifying crassitude, and greedy expediency. I cannot hope in so brief a survey to arrive at precise or definitive conclusions. But my exertions shall not be for naught if they can point out the need of desisting, for once and for all, from underrating the intellect of one denominated, more often by way of patronization than by way of affection or respect, as 'the old Gray poet,' 'the Solitary Singer,' or 'the Wound Dresser.'

In minor as well as decisively major aspects, there is an incredible identity in the lives and thoughts of Whitman and Nietzsche. Both were closely attached to their families by ties of affection and loyalty. Though not immune to woman's fascination either as bedfellow or companion, neither married. Whitman was very found of, and devoted to, his mother and brothers; Nietzsche, though he sporadically attempted to break away, was very much under the sway of his mother and sister. Whitman's love of music, particularly the opera, has furnished the materials for at least one book and several articles; Nietzsche's youthful passion for Wagner and his life-long attachment to music is

6

well attested. Both were filled with a measureless love of life, illimitable confidence in themselves, and irresistible personal magnetism. Each extolled the life of the senses and hymned death as the fairest festival of them all. Instead of bewailing man's sorrowful lot and his tragic mortality, Whitman and Nietzsche positively flung themselves into the affirmation of life and joy. In order that he might learn to love and live, man, they both taught, must refuse to despair. They were utopians who deprecated Utopias. They expounded a humanistic ethic that stressed effort and the will-to-utopia more than success and Utopia. In the face of hopes which betray and despair which debilitates, they asked man to emulate Achilles who is never oppressed by the future though he knows it holds an imminent doom. They anticipated Camus in urging man to serve simultaneously suffering (humanity) and beauty (art).

Both were inordinately addicted to self-portrayal and self-confessional. More clearly than in the case of most others, their writings reveal how large a portion of a writer's unfulfilled life finds expression and outlet in his work. Each liked to depict himself as bursting with vitality and well-being although neither was exceptionally robust. Whitman's rhapsodies to the sun, like those of D. H. Lawrence, were a consequence, in some measure no doubt, of his predisposition to be phthisic. During his late years, his health deteriorated rapidly and caused him untold mental and physical anguish. And Nietzsche was, although by necessity rather than

7

choice, practically a hypochondriac. He suffered from eyestrain, neuralgia, megrims, and epileptoid vertigo. His health, always delicate, underwent a severe setback during the second of his service stints in the medical corps. Interestingly enough, it was his Whitmanian sympathy for the wounded and desolate that led to the fatal neglect of his own health. Illness, for that matter, preoccupied both Whitman and Nietzsche. Quite naturally, they viewed it as the most palpable and damaging evidence of the mystery of evil. Both were acutely aware that no affirmation of life, no unconditional endorsement of existence, could stand up unless it reckoned with and disposed of the ugly actuality of disease.

Both were dignified, temperamental, dogged, energetic, eloquent, upright, fearless, noble, gracious, generous, perceptive, dedicated, prolix, reiterative, proud, didactic, eccentric, melodramatic, magnetic, grandiose, and egoistic. In addition, despite their façade of assuredness and bravado, they were introspective, shy, lonely, and insecure. Though diametrically opposed to what they taught, both wistfully reconciled themselves to achieving derring-do, not by feat-performing, but by writing. Each gave proof of a remarkable capability for sympathy and empathy. Each favored the metaphorical over the explicit; and each displayed a rare gift for brilliant and graphic utterance. Completely immersed in their self-appointed calling of prophet-seers, they spared no pains to win over an audience often absent or, at

8

best, indifferent if not hostile. Whitman's *outrè* garb, his fabulous catalogues which sometimes parody themselves, his erotic poems, his voicing of sentiments conventionally deemed indecorous and immature, made him an easy target for caricature. Nietzsche's reputation in his own lifetime suffered a similar fate. His hermit-like manner of living, his acrimonious rupture with Wagner, his strained relations with colleagues and acquaintances, his nervous collapse at Turin, his sister's irresponsible publication of his works with drastic editorializing and expedient deletions, unauthorized of course and designed to serve her own ends, obscured the true man and his thought for whatever carnival clown and specious doctrine one was of a mind and whim to accept as authentic. The crude, gutter-type abuse heaped upon Nietzsche far exceeded anything of a similar nature vented on Whitman, who has been dismissed more often as daft than as noxious. As Camus averred, we shall never cease indemnifying Nietzsche's tarnished luster. For that matter, nothing limns man's incorrigibleness and scholarship's vagaries so much as the misreading of an abiding love of life and humanity for flabby maudlinness in Whitman and for nordic ethnocentrism in Nietzsche.

Both proved reliable prophets of many of the external conflicts and inner distempers that plague our era. Whitman foresaw the increasing alienation and depersonalization technology would spawn. He warned that neither Democracy nor Industry could avail man if his spiritual wants were not given priority over the mechanical appurtenancies required for his material comfort. He was beforehand in anticipating the ills which would result from the folly of sexual Pharisaism, the fallibility of the ascertained knowledge we call Science, the affinity between tyrant and priest, the crude fetishism and magic we revere as sacred convention and enshrined law. Nietzsche foretold a number of the excesses of the twentieth century by lucidly reasoning that man's cultural and ethical heritage had hardly fortified him for a godless way of life. Nietzsche correctly foresaw that, when confronted with the Kierkegaardian abyss, the few would negotiate the leap, but the many would cringe and would soon be in the clutches of the ruthless and unprincipled, whose strength derives from the obedience they exact from those in whom the need to obey is greater even than the will to survive. Both cautioned against the modern evils of despair and debilitation of will. They appreciated the fact that, unless man remained true to himself, unless he retained his faith in life, unless he could find meaningful goals to pursue, he would plunge into a twilight world of meaningless shadows which represent nothing the heart can yearn for, nothing the mind may delight in, nothing the spirit can cherish and exalt. They besought man never to confound love and justice; never to sanction equality when it was prepared to sacrifice personal expression to collectivity. They wisely perceived that the lonely crowd is not lonely; that only the individual indistinguishable from the crowd and desolate when

10

not amid the crowd is lonely. They insisted man distinguish sharply between the real and the ideal, and not permit himself to become the victim of an ideal all his faith and love could never realize.

They were positive that darkness as well as light is bound up with the life of every organism; that in creation tiger and lamb are inextricably mingled; that man's life has its sunsets and its sunrises. They summoned the testimony of biology and psychology to bolster their case that differentiation and conflict were requisites as well as characteristics of life. To them, the only original sin was the sin against life, the sin entailed by the fear of pleasure, laughter, and death. Both professed to a belief in natural immortality; they asserted that the man who consummates his life dies his death triumphantly, without bitterness, without regret. They pictured death as a phoenix perishing in its own flames, solemnly saying no when there was no longer time for saying yes, willing its destruction as it had willed its creation, and as it would will its re-creation. Always their most aroused polemic was against the teachers of gravity and graves, against necrophilia and necrolatry. They held with Zarathustra that those who do not laugh sufficiently are incapable of loving selflessly. Each diagnosed the malady of his contemporaries as fear, and the despair consequent upon this fear. As Nietzsche wrote in the third essay of *The Genealogy of Morals:*

We can no longer conceal from ourselves what exactly it is that this whole process of willing, inspired by the ascetic ideal, signifies – this hatred of humanity, of animality, of inert matter; this loathing of the senses, of reason even; this fear of beauty and happiness; this longing to escape from illusion, change, becoming, death, and from longing itself. It signifies, let us have the courage to face it, a will to nothingness, a revulsion from life, a rebellion against the principal conditions of living.

To combat this form of suicidal anorexia, Whitman and Nietzsche commanded man to leave off imbibing the lotus weed, to stop wishing for the flower without the stalk, to cast aside the barren *esse* and to clasp to his bosom the fertile *vivere*. They perceived astutely that the worst tragedy of herd prescriptiveness would be not stolid mediocrity but a petrifying uniformity that would imperil life itself. Both preferred vehement paroxysms of Promethean defiance to passive and pacific babblings of hopeless apathy. Though neither would have subscribed to Gide's type of gratuitous hedonism, both would have said nautch girls promote life more than scrofulous monastics.

Whitman's occasional misgivings which tempted him to believe that all of what is designated objective reality might be Maya would have been contemptuously relegated by Nietzsche to the realm of sententious rigmarole. And Whitman's belief in the eternal real life to come would hardly have received a more favorable hearing at the Nietzschean assizes. Notwithstanding, both agreed that it behooved man to affirm life by affirming self. In the message they proclaimed to the world, they implored man to reject whatever was not self-created, whatever subordinated, subdued, or suppressed self. Their

12

writings are a complete *vade mecum* on individualism. They called upon man to forge new standards
and goals for himself, employing as criterion only
what he had experienced as fit and apt in the
microcosm of self. They called upon man to re-
trieve from programmed electronic circuitry a portion of his instinctual spontaneity. They called
upon man to sally forth in his own and not in a
borrowed or convention-enforced identity. They
believed tradition and the past either had to
subserve the present or be superseded. Man must
first be shorn of vain dreams, they said, before he
can help realize the dream of the future; like
Shelley's West Wind, man must first be a destroyer
before he is ready to become a creator. They felt it
was incumbent upon man to serve truth un-
waveringly and to deify the vital instead of seeking
to eschew life through aesthetic or ascetic contem-
plation. And, scrupulously faithful to their own
preachment, they sought no reader who would not
refute them whenever he failed to confirm their
teachings through himself.

Unlike Nietzsche, Whitman was perfectly at
home with the supernatural and the mystical; he
had no difficulty in embracing simultaneously both
the transcendental and the naturalistic. Yet, like
Nietzsche, he was always urging man to find his
incentive for living, life's goal and meaning, in the
joy that is effable, in the grass that can be scented,
in the hand that can be grasped, in the oenomel of
perishable grapes. Keat's bittersweet reconcili-
ation, arrived at via the Grecian urn's tale and the

13

immortal bird's song, is transfigured into a splendid
assertion of vitality in Whitman and Nietzsche.
The *taedium vitae* of the cynic and the *carpe diem*
of the hedonist are alike brusquely brushed aside by
Whitman and Nietzsche. For they endeavor to
bring man to an unflinching total awareness. They
want him to stand unafraid and undismayed before
the unbearable actuality. They want him to over-
master his panic impulse for oblivion through an
escape out of life or through a phrenetic submersion
in life. They want man to take upon himself the
full burden of responsibility and freedom; they
want him, like Sisyphus, to heft the rock and trudge
wearily albeit gladly up the incline braced by the
very knowledge that human struggle can only end
in provisional victories that will ceaselessly be
questioned.

"It requires great strength to be able to live and
forget how far life and injustice are one," Nietzsche
wrote in one of his earliest works, *The Use & Abuse
of History*. Nevertheless both he and Whitman
realized man must learn to do precisely this on pain
of extinction. Resentment and revenge, they logically reasoned, were incompatible with saying yes
to life. Man must oppose with might and main all
that degraded him as a living being and a source of
life. Man must unceasingly strive against life-
denying ennui and against the life-negation of ad-
judication. He must emerge from his Cimmerian
despair and his Empedoclean dudgeon to the full
stature of his existential being. He must refrain
from substituting knowledge for wisdom, progress

14

for truth, justice for love, morality for vitality. He must posit life's patent absurdity and fortuity, and then derive from the self-same absurdity and fortuity the resolution to embrace them jubilantly as the destiny he neither can nor wishes to propitiate. Man's life must be built on the further side of despair, rather than on the far side of a mythical paradise. His hosannas must be directed to the palpably biotic and not to cenotaphs. He must render unto life the things that are life's and refuse tribute to all else.

Whitman and Nietzsche followed Emerson in saying that speculation was a poor substitute for life's dictionary. One may object that they did not follow themselves what they undertook to teach others, but one would have to agree that they did preach the need for subordinating ratiocination to living. Both withered with their scorn the *ipse dixit* which from Parmenides through Descartes to Hegel defined being in terms of thought (*Cogito, ergo sum*). Both would have found equally, if not more, valid D. H. Lawrence's 'I don't think I am. I know I am!' They did not repudiate one aspect of being in the name of another. But they did declare that, in order to satisfy the entire man, reason should be animated by emotion. They distrusted and contemned the jaded idlers in the garden of apodictic knowledge. They jolly well put in their place those dialectical wiseacres who, failing to explicate the fact of knowledge by the fact of existence, equivocate and attribute to knowledge the power of creating reality. They pointed out that the rational is not necessarily more veridical than the non-rational; that authentic knowing is largely interpretation. In "A Song for Occupations," Whitman wrote:

All architecture is what you do to it when you look upon it, (Did you think it was in the white or gray stone? or in the arches and cornices?)
All music is what awakes from you when you are reminded by the instruments.

They regarded scientific objectivity as delusory, and viewed the "passionate intensity" of the scientists as clear indication the latter, lacking faith in the old convictions, had neither the courage nor the sight and wisdom to formulate new convictions. For Nietzsche, science was "the very *anxiety* that springs from having no ideal, the suffering from the *lack* of a great love, the discontent with an enforced moderation." Whitman, usually more conciliatory though not always more catholic, stood ever ready to concede science and scientists had their appointed place in the general scheme of things and would play crucial roles in moulding the glowing future he confidently foretold. Yet he invariably qualified all such concessions by remarking that the hush of astral presences, the intuition of the mantic bard, the sibylline scintilla of poetic frenzy, the mystic electricity of human touch excelled all scientific and philosophic lore. In *Specimen Days*, he wrote:

While the contributions which German Kant and Fichte and Schelling and Hegel have bequeathed to humanity

16

– and which English Darwin has also in his field – are indispensable to the erudition of America's future, I should say that all of them, and the best of them, when compared with the lightning flashes and flights of the old prophets and *exaltés*, the spiritual poets and poetry of all lands (as in the Hebrew Bible), there seems to be, nay certainly is, something lacking – something cold, a failure to satisfy the deepest emotions of the soul – a want of living glow, fondness, warmth, which the old *exaltés* and poets supply, and which the keenest modern philosophers so far do not.

Several decades before Werner Heisenberg, Whitman and Nietzsche questioned the principle of causality and surmised that there could be a nondeterminist understanding of exterior reality. They held that a true knowledge of existence entailed an understanding of the interrelation of the subjective and the objective. Art as well as external reality, they contended, could be cognized relatively not absolutely; true cognition required cognition of creator and spectator in addition to cognition of observed object. In *The Genealogy of Morals*, Nietzsche put the matter as follows:

There is only a seeing from a perspective, only a "knowing" from a perspective, and the *more* emotions we express over a thing, the *more* eyes, different eyes, we train on the same thing, the more complete will be our 'idea' of that thing, our "objectivity". But the elimination of the will altogether, the switching off of the emotions all and sundry, granted that we could do so, what! would not that be called intellectual *castration*?

Observed reality for Whitman and Nietzsche was coextensive with the observer's coenesthesia. Their

unwavering trust in man's inner resources convinced them that reality could be as restricted or as
limitless as man's power to envisage it. In a verse
that might be construed as a faint precursor of
Nietzsche's notorious dictum on his hypothetical
anguish at not being a deity in a theoretically
deistic cosmos, Whitman exclaimed:

Dazzling and tremendous how quick the sun-rise would
kill me,
If I could not now and always send sun-rise out of me.

Whitman and Nietzsche were not prepared to make
a burnt offering of the living on the sacrificial altar
of the men of the future. Most of the time, their
emphasis was on the precious present, on the
inviolable sanctity of the here and now in opposition
to the future. They had little liking for those whose
predisposition to millenial fantasies and hookah
visions of superterrestrial felicities blinded them
to the distinction between the factitious and the
factual. But Whitman's and Nietzsche's Beatitudes
to the palpitating, palpable present do not partake
in the least of hedonistic nihilism or cynical sen-
sualism. Their unconditional endorsement of existence – *"Lux, mea crux; crux, mea lux!"* as Nietzsche rapturously expressed it in his notebooks –
specifically indicted nihilism and prominently featured a halcyon future peopled by superior men
who would be exempt from the majority of debilitating fears and hopes, who would be supremely
confident yet not arrogant in their absolute individualism and self-reliance. Both Whitman and   **18**

Nietzsche prophesied an era in which great men
– men, that is, who had achieved self-conquest and
therby attained to true freedom (*"...befreit der
Mensch sich, der sich überwindet,"* as Goethe expressed the notion common to Socrates and Emerson among others,) – would be the products of
conscious human direction and human will rather
than fortunate accidents. After all, a genuine and
abiding affection for what is would naturally eventuate in the hope and determination that it be
perpetuated or improved. The hope, which springs
eternally even in breasts that scoff at supernal
rewards, incorporates the will-to-utopia – the instinctual predisposition not only for the preservation but also for the betterment of man's condition. A romantic idealist, like Whitman and
Nietzsche, must persuade himself that, since man is
able to, he will wish to improve himself spiritually
and psychologically, not to mention physically, in
order that he and his issue may discover, pursue,
and achieve higher goals than those scrabbled after
by the mongrel conformist, the fulsome timeserver,
the craven lickspit, the abject anonymity never by
passion quite possessed. (Both recall the wistful
Don whose magnificently ineffectual sallies in the
defense and promulgation of what was best and
noblest instead of safest and easiest made him appear ludicrous and inane to a wrongheaded world.)
The romantic idealist feels that only in this way
can man fulfill the destiny to which he is not called
but to which he should, nonetheless, be committed
by his noblest parts.

19

Whitman and Nietzsche entertained great ex-
pectations of this imminent noontide of superior
earthlings: when the total recuperation of man's
humanity would be effectuated; when the jettison-
ing of herd-forged halters and gelid interdictions
would arrest the fatal atrophy of man's will and
restore to him the wisdom of precultural existence;
when direct reformation of individual life would
pave the way for far-reaching social, political, and
artistic improvements; when freedom would be
both the parent and offspring of personal responsibility. For these superior beings would possess, as
Nietzsche tells us in *The Will to Power*, "an overflow of energy for beauty, bravery, culture, and
manners even for the most abstract thought; a
yea-saying race which would be able to allow itself
every kind of great luxury – strong enough to be
able to dispense with the tyranny of the imperatives
of virtue, rich enough to be in no need of economy
or pedantry." Their banners would proclaim not
vae victis but *amor vincit omnia*. Such men would
easily cope with what Heidegger, in his interpretation of Hölderlin, terms the double negation, the
no-more of the gods that have fled and the not-yet
of the god who is coming. They would formulate
what D. H. Lawrence in his discussion of Whitman
termed a "morality of actual living, not of salvation." Their bible would be a critique of all prevailing values and virtues; their ambition would
be to become, through self-knowledge and self-
determination, their authentic selves. Their society
would be the very antithesis of that in which   20

anonymity is the most prized virtue, numerical strength the decisive factor, and majority opinion the divine oracle. This "new race dominating previous ones, and grander far, with new contests, / New politics, new literatures and religions, new inventions and arts" ("Starting From Paumanok") would admit no speculation whose soundness could not be circumstantiated in vivo. Its main concern would be essential existence, not conceptualized essences. Its pantheon would be life; and worshippers would worship by learning to live wholly by tellurian precepts. The great individualists comprising this exemplary race would rely on their own inner resources to combat the temptations of total, personal suzerainty and the noxious arguments of nihilism. Imbued with the joy of the brave, the laughter of the wise, and the mirth of the vitally alive, they would scatter "for good the cloud that hung so long, that weigh'd so long upon the mind of man, / The doubt, suspicion, dread, of gradual, certain decadence of man" ("Thou Mother With Thy Equal Brood").

Lest oversimplification be carried too far, it may prove prudent to hint at the differences in Carlyle's, Nietzsche's, and Whitman's conceptions of the great man or hero. Carlyle's hero subserves history since his function, conceived largely in utilitarian terms, is to avert or dispel chaos and anarchy. Carlyle understood history as the biographical records of great men. Nietzsche's hero is his own justification for being; his greatness derives not from his utility to history but from his intrinsic worth.

21

Sanction for his actions does not proceed from any legal, divine, rationalistic, materialistic, or pragmatic ethic. He is a law unto himself, a "Roman Caesar with Christ's soul," in Nietzsche's phrase (*The Will to Power*). Whitman's hero conforms closely to Emerson's fearless, self-reliant individualist who does not hesitate to place his trust in whim and who laughs to scorn the restraints of prudence. The principal difference is that Whitman's hero is free of all Emersonian prudishness, inhibitions, and delicacy:

> I announce the great individual, fluid as Nature, chaste, affectionate, compassionate, fully arm'd.
>
> .   .   .
>
> I announce myriads of youths, beautiful, gigantic, sweet-blooded,
> I announce a race of splendid and savage old men.
>
> ("So Long!")

But both Whitman and Nietzsche would have agreed with Emerson that there can be "no interval between greatness and meanness. When the spirit is not master of the world, then it is its dupe" ("Heroism"). Carlyle saw his hero as the ruler of subjects, Nietzsche as the teacher of disciples, and Whitman as a Camerado tramping the open road hand in hand with other Camerados.

Both Whitman and Nietzsche, it is curious to note, took exception to Carlyle's notion of heroism. In *Specimen Days*, Whitman pays tribute to Carlyle as Old Testament-type of prophet, and even grants that Carlyle's withering onslaughts against America

22

and Americans are in some measure justified. At
the same time, however, he deprecates the Scotchman's oligarchic preferences: "The great masses of
humanity stand for nothing – at least nothing but
nebulous raw material; only the big planets and
shining suns for him." Nietzsche angrily discounts
the allegation that his Superman theory owes anything to "the 'hero-worship' of that great counter-
feiter against his own knowledge and will, Carlyle."
More constructively, in the sentences preceding
this choice vituperation from *Ecce Homo*, Nietzsche
explains his Supermen are not 'modern' men, nor
'good' men, nor Christian saints, nor nihilists. They
cannot be produced by institutionalized Christianity, nor by the doctrine of Progress, nor through
Darwinian evolution. (Nietzsche, like Shaw, was a
Lamarckian.) The Superman is best exemplified,
Nietzsche continues, by Zarathustra, an "'idealistic' type of a higher kind of man, half 'saint,' half
'genius'." Nietzsche's Superman might suggest to
some the Superman of G. B. Shaw. But the German
philosopher was distinctly a-political (possibly anti-
political) and would have looked upon the Irish
playwright's advocacy of intelligence without cor-
poreity as daft. Nietzsche could espouse rationality
readily when oppugning the faith of a creed founded on rank superstition and cretinous illusionism.
Yet he was equally vehement in attacking any
scientific rationalism that appropriated to itself the
meaningless rightness of absolute authority.

In a splenetic moment, Nietzsche cursed John
Stuart Mill as a blockhead. But he, no less than

Whitman, seems to have agreed with Mill's contention that freedom for man requires more than civil liberties; that true freedom requires unimpeded fulfillment. Nietzsche's aristocratic contempt for the herd might appear diametrically opposed to Whitman's democratic compassion for the masses. But such is not the case. Nietzsche despised the herd as herd not the herd as individual men; he was of Swift's not Timon's mind. It is to the undifferentiated many that Zarathustra tries, though in vain, to impart his preachment that man must overcome himself. At the outset of his katabasis, down from the mountain, back to man, Zarathustra is stopped by a hermit who tells him the mass of men are sleepers who will neither listen nor awaken and the punishment reserved for sleep-disturbers is the stake. He remarks that, after ten years of solitude, Zarathustra is rejuvenated, his eyes bright and clear, and his expression no longer filled with disgust at men's ways. The hermit is at a loss to understand why Zarathustra is not content to remain in the forest and desires to go to man again. Zarathustra answers simply that he loves mankind. Nor is there any reason to question Nietzsche's compassion for his fellow man. It might be argued that, had he known Manhattan's human droppings at first hand, he would have been, unlike Whitman, appreciably less sanguine regarding man's capabilities for self-improvement. But Nietzsche's voluminous writings on human nature, human motivation, and human achievement prove beyond dispute that, though he knew

24

more of human failings and vices than Whitman ever saw or imagined, he was not a whit less optimistic than his American counterpart regarding man and man's destiny. And, where Whitman and Nietzsche are concerned, faith such as this denotes love rather than blindness, perversity, or worse. No one can devote his entire life's work to impressing upon man his great potential for improving himself, developing himself, and rising superior to the limitations of his nature unless he is imbued with a deep and abiding love of humanity. Savage laceration, incessant adjuration, and reiterated assertions of confidence can proceed only from a heart that cares – often in spite of itself. Nietzsche more intellectually high-strung than Whitman and all too familiar with the stings and stinks of academic pismires and polecats, was understandably less skilled in patience and tolerance than Whitman. Working out of the chamber of a hypochondriac-hermit-invalid and leading the existence of the inhabitant of such a cell, it would have been very easy and natural for him to have embraced that same nihilism he predicated as the cornerstone of his philosophy of the affirmation of life's joy and anguish without transcendence. Ignored, maligned, irritatingly and gratuitously misconstrued, he never wavered in his crusade to help man disengage himself from all that was dead and deleterious and help him form a vital connection with all that was creative and made people aware of what it meant to be an existing individual. In view of the often blind, inconsidered, and blanket arraignments of

25

the herd that have been so popular in our era and have established huge reputations for their authors, the wonder is not that Whitman and Nietzsche, who anticipated all the arguments against uniformity and conformity, despaired many times of reclaiming a generation that had sold its birthright of intrinsic curiosity for a mass of pre-digested knowledge capsules and bartered its artistic sense for a mess of potted palms, but that they should have persevered in their abiding faith in the human race. If one bears in mind Alexander Hamilton's notorious albeit basically accurate estimate of the people, for whom the Roman had the aptest of terms, one may wonder why anyone, aside from manifest psychotics like Moses and Marx, would devote his life's energies in their behalf. Is the Messiah complex universal – latent in all? Or does it manifest itself with pronounced strength in certain temperaments? Are those who labor under severe handicaps, or encounter rejection, failure, insult, mistreatment, abuse, injustice early in life, more inclined to transmogrify their misfortune, whether real or imaginary, into a universal agony of Promethean proportions, and, with a grandiloquent gesture, shoulder the world's ills, and pen a gospel of salvation? The role of religion in the lives of Whitman and Nietzsche will help suggest some of the answers.

Each was reared in a pious household, and, to the end, each retained an ingrained sense of religious ethos. Whitman is radically unorthodox by the criteria of most denominations, and there is no

26

doubt that, like Hegel, he felt religion should be popular, not clerical, humane, not otherworldly, creative, not ascetic, joyous, not gloomy, democratic, not sectarian. Christ's teachings of brotherhood and love are written large on every page he wrote. Like Emerson, however, he had many reservations regarding Ministers and Churches; like the great teacher of self-reliance, he, also, believed it was the duty of everyone to seek a direct relationship with God himself. Whitman found god in nature and in man; in man's flesh and in man's spirit; in a leaf of grass and in a Brooklyn ferry; in the passionate kisses exchanged in a hayloft and in the solemn beads of the holy hermit; in the face of President Lincoln and in the countenance of the common prostitute; in the benign physiognomy of good and in the evil leer of evil. Whitman's God was ubiquitous, omnipresent, and immanent in life. Though often conceptualized anthropomorphically, invoked in the conventional manner, and imaged as the Camerado hospitably welcoming new arrivals at Heaven's Portals, Whitman even more often equates or identifies God with Self and/or Creation, and, by this convenient equation or identification, dispenses with God altogether. This may appear an unwarranted assumption, but one eventually becomes exasperated with Emerson's and Whitman's dubious logic which enables them to be blithely and supremely smug in their reliance on Self because Self is God. If one chooses to say his actions are correct and right and good because they are so in his own eyes and because they are conducive to his

27

well being – that is one thing. For, if there is a discrepancy between his thoughts on these matters and the thoughts of others, such a discrepancy will very soon be brought to his attention and he will be confronted with Thoreau's choice. But it is an entirely different matter when one claims Divine endorsement for an act of caprice. Or is it? Emerson does not consider the possibility of a conflict between God-Reliance and Self-Reliance because he could not conceive of a clash of interests between the Oversoul and the Self. Many, however, might feel such a position to be a flagrant evasion of a real and valid question. Emerson would retort that a responsible and conscientious person could never be misled by the infallible mentor within him. And, here, alas, Emerson would be ruthlessly impaled by the relentless inquisitor. For where, indeed, is individualism when, in the interests of being responsible, one must consult the wishes and welfare of others, and, in the interests of conscience, one must check with the mores, ethics, and codes of his society? If Emerson could reassure himself by pointing out that his preachment was for the individual who was sensible and knew well Aristotle's teachings, and not for crackpot anarchists and radical malcontents, others were not so easily satisfied. Neither Thoreau nor Whitman repudiated their master, but both were prepared to carry individualism, off the lecture platform, much further than Emerson was. There are passages in which Whitman exalts the individual to the status of sole deity, others wherein he acknowledges and

28

welcomes nether impulses scarcely of reputable origin, and still others in which individualism finds triumphant expression in the celebration of the sexual urge. Endowed with a remarkably keen pagan receptivity to nature and a richly sensual temperament – both of which were intensified by his paradoxically ecstatic yet anguished anticipation of death – Whitman, at his most spontaneous, characteristic, and individualistic, laid more stress on the fraternity of suffering by which men are united, and on the magic of love by which they are transported, than he did on supernal panaceas. Since his principal objective was to rediscover the values of life and happiness, Whitman would have been prepared to join Nietzsche in prizing life more than god, and, with some qualifications, just as ready as Nietzsche to set individual freedom above religion, ethics, and state. Perhaps Whitman would not have been prepared to concur, but he most surely would have strongly sympathized, with Camus' conviction that life is the only necessary good. At the same time, Whitman, unlike Nietzsche, did not think a belief in a transcendent order or immutable entity entailed a devaluation of the temporal order. Together with Heraclitus and Nietzsche, Whitman was prepared to accept change as a fundamental fact of existence, yet he still recognized order and harmony as immanent in the universe and, for the most part, rejected Nietzsche's cosmic fortuity. Whitman's mysticism consisted of a few Buddhistic notions, an unusual sensitivity of intuitive perception, and a belief "in what," as he

says in *Specimen Days,* "cannot be defined to the
intellectual part, or to calculation." As did the
states in the Civil War, he saw body and soul dis-
solving and dividing at death only to be reconciled
and become united in a higher unity. Whitman's
mysticism sought to give to quotidian experience
the stamp of the eternal, rather than to preach the
cessation of all effort until the great sabbath of
sabbaths. Whitman saw no contradiction – and
would not have been perturbed if he had – between
his fidelity to the present and presence and his twin
vision of a superterrestrial and telluric reign of
perfect felicity.

Most, if not the whole, of Nietzsche's thought
stems from his violent reaction to Christianity.
Whatever topic he may be discussing at the moment – Greek tragedy, the Will to Power, the
Eternal Recurrence, Morality, Psychology, Supermen, War, Science, Good and Evil, Wagner –
sooner or later, he will introduce the topic of
Christianity. Born the son of a minister, he spent
his life composing one of the most formidable
arraignments and one of the most thersitical denunciations of institutionalized and historical
Christianity on record. His entire philosophy, in
fact, can be understood as an attempt to re-evaluate
all values, to understand life, and to define man's
goals, without reference to, and in defiance of,
Christian precepts, institutions, and creeds. It can
be said he anticipated Freud, Marx, and the
Existentialists by foreseeing the day when man
would have to find the courage to live without god

30

or perish. Nietzsche's self-appointed mission was to rescue man from the darkling plain; to indicate to him the wherewithal to create Man-God to replace God-Man. The undertaking, of course, was an enormous if not an impossible one. But an even more formidable impediment was the uncertainty that assailed Nietzsche regarding his finding a solution and perhaps even regarding the rightness of his course of action. Too often Nietzsche is misleadingly portrayed as vaunting himself a God like Caligula, gleefully cavorting with the Devil as he spouts all manner of blasphemies and impieties, or detachedly, with the meticulous precision of a mathematician, razing Christianity to rubble. Actually, however, Nietzsche suffered untold agonies as he sought to accept emotionally as well as rationally the fact of God's death and, at the same time, circumvent nihilism. The fanatical zeal with which he threw himself into his labors readily reminds one of the religious frenzy of an Old Testament prophet and the supreme dedication of a religious leader. The Zarathustra we meet descending from the mountain forest to travel to men's cities is strongly suggestive of the holy men who after their sojourn in the wilderness are ready to commence their ministry. The vitriolic vehemence with which Nietzsche launches his diatribes against the doctrines of Christianity testifies not so much to a precocious atheism as it does to the artist's anger at the deprecation of beauty; the vitalist's protest against etiolation; the naturalist's objection to considering real what is abstract; the humanist's

31

rage against the gulling and depreciation of man; the personalist's indignation against the suppression and mutilation of man's individuality. A rabid individualist and brilliantly original thinker like Nietzsche would naturally rebel against the suffocating traditionalism, the benighted dogmatism, and the inane absolutism of Christianity. One should remember that Kierkegaard, Hegel, and many others assailed the Christianity of the Church on much the same grounds that Nietzsche did. It may also be helpful to remember that Nietzsche was a fervent Hellenist and that he believed the Greeks in their marriage of the Dionysiac and Apollonian had intuited earth's aim and man's hope infinitely better than Europe had under Christianity. Like that of so many other bitter foes of Pauline Christianity, Nietzsche's criticism of Christ himself was relatively mild. Even though he hysterically attacked Schopenhauer for elevating pity to the stature of the supreme virtue, even though he pictured God in one place as having died through his pity for man, and, even though, in *Zarathustra*, pity for man is represented as the last great temptation Zarathustra (who, disappointed with his mission to man, has returned to his mountain retreat, with a serpent and a lion as companions) must avoid succumbing to, Nietzsche was too filled with the milk of human kindness not to feel for all suffering things as tender a love as felt by Christ and Whitman. At times, Nietzsche, interpreting Christ in his own terms, commends Him for repudiating tradition and preaching the glad evangel

32

of personalism: "Salvation by faith means that the heart alone, not knowledge, can bring happiness. The incarnation of God suggests that man shall not seek salvation in infinity but shall found his heaven on earth." At other times, Nietzsche condemned Christ for his passivity and likened him to Dostoievski's idiot Prince. Especially disturbing to Nietzsche was the death on the cross which he construed as a renunciation of the this-worldly and which he contrasted unfavorably to the shrieking dismemberment of Dionysus. To Nietzsche, it seemed that Christ embraced death as a release from life and that his death was hence a negation of life's earthly cycle, whereas Dionysus submitted to death as a phase of life's cycle that he might be regenerated eternally. At still other times, Nietzsche identified himself with Christ, pointing out that Christ was a self-proclaimed destroyer of morality and that Christ saw himself as beyond good and evil. During his mental illness, Nietzsche signed himself not only as Dionysus but also as The Crucified. It was perhaps his last pathetic effort to tell a still-incredulous world that what he had always sought was man's salvation. It may also hint at the profound depths of Nietzsche's perturbation as he sought frantically, with the frenzied logic of an artist's emotion rather than mathematical induction, to substitute for Christian immortality his semi-mystical doctrine of eternal recurrence, and to shift cosmic responsibility and rule from God to Man through his visionary concept of Superman.

33 It would appear that dissolution of identity was

an intolerable thought both to Whitman and Nietzsche. To Whitman, it evidently was a greater bugbear than physical infirmity and no doubt accounts in large measure for his anxiety to establish that death is a phase of life's cycle rather than a termination of it. To exorcise the adamant finality of the arch invisible fear, Whitman summons to the aid of his poetic alchemy every available source – theological, theosophic, and even scientific. He espoused eidolons – Platonic archetypes which always have been and which always will be. From Emerson, he appropriated the notion that every human being is a portion of the Divine Substance, out of which he issues and into which he is reintromitted – a notion recognizable in the organic outgoing-ingoing metaphor so prominent in his poems. He saw God immanent in all creation, and believed that all things, including God, continually tended toward the supreme repository, the All. Influenced by Buddhism, he believed in countless former and future births and deaths of himself as avatar of eternity. He believed in the immortality of the body through the perpetuity of life and in the immortality of the soul through the continuance of identity. (Buddhism declares that life can never die out entirely since the universe will always be and, even if life died out on our planet, the conditions that engendered it here would reoccur either here or elsewhere.) He believed his very being was somehow inspissated in his verse, and that he could materialize at the reader's touch:

34

Camerado, this is no book,
Who touches this touches a man,
(Is it night? are we here together alone?)
It is I you hold and who holds you,
I spring from the pages into your arms – decease calls me
    forth.

Less multifarious than Whitman, at least in this
one respect, Nietzsche allayed his anxiety, as we
have indicated, by his myth of eternal return – his
version of the Pythagorean ἀνακύκλοσις, an ancient doctrine often associated with mystical and
theosophical movements, which Nietzsche apparently felt was tenable within a naturalistic frame
of reference. Nietzsche's perpetual cycles theory
held that no event is unique, that no event occurs
for once and for all. Every event has occurred,
occurs, and will continue to occur *in perpetuo*. The
same individuals have appeared, appear, and reappear at every return of the cycle upon itself.
Duration can be cognized only in terms of periodi-
city. The same situations are reproduced that have
already been produced in previous cycles and will
be reproduced in subsequent cycles – *ad infinitum*.
From his version of the myth, Nietzsche excluded
the Platonic definition of time as the moving image
of unmoving eternity. And, of course, he also
excluded the corollary to this, *viz.*, that the perfect
and ultimate divine goal of circular motion is
absolute immobility. In Nietzsche's cosmos, time
is infinite, but energy is determinate.

    Nietzsche enhanced his belief by providing for
the exercise of free will within the very bastion of

necessitarianism. Thus he could reject all idealism of the archetype-prototype variety, and, at the same time, contend man makes of himself what he wills. For the fact that man cannot make of himself anything he has not been and will be again does not prevent his making himself any one of an infinite number of things. There is no contradiction in demanding the creation of superior men and the reoccurrence of all precisely as it is now. Nietzsche's eternal return postulates periodic but not seriatim occurrence; all repeats but there is no specific (or, what amounts to the same thing, no predetermined) sequence of repetition. The different possibilities in sequences are innumerable. Man can create himself and his immediate future. And in this knowledge and in the knowledge that identity is forever, reside man's freedom and joy. This twin knowledge is, furthermore, man's only and best mithridate against the sickness unto death, the *angst* and angoisse which assail man when he realizes he is an accident and that creation is a fortuitous concourse of atoms.

Although it might be said that, in one sense, Whitman and Nietzsche were anti-romantic in refusing to confound the real with the ideal or life with dream, they displayed many of the romanticist's traits: through their faith in the vital instinct; through their iconoclasm; through their delirious eulogies and renitent denunciations; through their rampant egoism; through their libertarianism. Both sought to be representative of their times and to surmount the problems of their times in them-

36

selves. Both would have consented to have Kierkegaard's words serve as epigraph to their works:
"My whole life is an epigram calculated to make
people aware."

Both have been dismissed as Goethe dismissed
Byron: 'When he reflects, he is a child.' In his
introduction to the Signet edition of *Leaves of
Grass*, Gay Wilson Allen quotes T. S. Eliot as saying:
"When Whitman speaks of the lilacs or the mock-
ing-bird, his theories and beliefs drop away like a
needless pretext." And Santayana, in his *Egotism
in German Philosophy*, spoke banteringly of Nietzsche's "genial imbecility" and "boyish blasphemies"
– epithets endorsed by Bertrand Russell, epithets of
the kind that greeted almost every edition of the
Leaves in Whitman's lifetime and several decades
later. Both, moreover, took an especial delight –
which can be understood as Emersonian greatness
just as readily as imbecility – in twitting sluggish-
witted panglozers, in assuming the prophet's
mantle, and in outraging the unco guid.

Whitman cannot match the urbane irony and
scintillating wit of Nietzsche. Nor is he capable of
the clownish impishness, the Tybalt leaps and
thrusts, the Mercutio ripostes – all embraced in the
virtuosity of Nietzsche's epigrams. But both authors sound alike when they unclench the floodgates
of their speech and, like the chiliasts, alternately
chide, beseech, and inspirit all who choose to hear.
Whitman and Zarathustra are either verbally
scourging the money-changers from the Temple, or
37   sermonizing on the Mount of Olives. Like the

waters of a subterranean mountain stream suddenly surfacing with explosive force, their words seethe forth in fast thick pants, rush pell mell in spuming torrent along a straightaway stretch of the channel bed, and, then, along a meandering bend in the channel, gradually slow to a lulling murmur. The reader cannot choose but hear.

To appreciate fully the correspondence in the ideas of Whitman and Nietzsche, one can do no better than to read both authors together in their entirety. By way of an aid, rather than an exhaustive collation, the more salient parallels together with corroborative quotations are enumerated in the following pages.

MERIT OF CONTRADICTION

Even a cursory indagation will disclose the crucial role played by contradiction in moulding the thought of Whitman and Nietzsche. Whether as a weapon of rhetoric or a decorative trope, whether as biotic law or quintessential signifier of life's myriad-faceted mystery, both writers found paradox congenial. They insisted that, in order to be uninhibitedly forthright and genuinely individualistic, one must liberate himself from prudential consistency. They agreed that, if one were to exist as an independent human entity who refused to enfeoff his individuality to institutionalism, one must be prepared to contradict himself and others freely and fearlessly. They heartily subscribed to Emerson's dictum – "Speak what you think now in hard words and tomorrow speak what tomorrow thinks in hard words again, though it contradict every thing you said today." And, there is little doubt they would have seconded Jaspers in asserting that freedom can neither be defined nor attain cogency without contradiction.

To Whitman and Nietzsche, contradiction and opposition were condiments that lent zest to existence. Contradiction was the cosmic diastole; it imbued life with meaning in the manner death defined life and rendered it precious. Contradiction was a measure of, and a safeguard for, dissentience. Without it, stultifying uniformity and gelid inanition would entrench themselves irremediably. Contradiction promoted life, being the lifeblood of master spirits. Only craven bezonians who, though covertly coveting, lacked the hardihood to pluck, deemed life's nectareous sweets sour grapes. Only clapperclawers of human existence disparaged contradiction. The man who trusted himself to the extent of mastering himself was perfectly at ease before his inconsistencies, nay, prided himself upon them:

Do I contradict myself?
Very well then I contradict myself,
(I am large, I contain multitudes.)
"Song of Myself," p. 68

Product and avatar of all past beings, representative and spokesman for all present beings, inseminator and forerunner of all future beings, Whitman incorporates in himself all human traits and their opposites, all human qualities and their counterparts, all theses and their antitheses, all assertions and their negations, all declarations and their denials. In such a commodious cosmos, no contradiction can prove of serious consequence for, in such a cosmos, as Whitman had learned from studying Emerson's concept of the Oversoul, discord and disunity are temporary states, mere harbingers of the ultimate condition of perfect harmony and oneness. In the last analysis, therefore, no evil was so inveterate and malignant as to be beyond rehabilitation, no contrariety so incorrigible as to be beyond rectification:

We stand amid time beginningless and endless, we stand
    amid evil and good,
All swings around us, there is as much darkness as light,
The very sun swings itself and its system of planets around
    us,

40

Its sun, and its again, all swing around us.

As for me, (torn, stormy, amid these vehement days,)
I have the idea of all, and am all and believe in all,
I believe materialism is true and spiritualism is true, I
    reject no part.
"With Antecedents," p. 176

Whitman was *beyond* contradiction in the same
sense in which Nietzsche held that the superior
being was beyond good and evil; he was not duped
by bigotry's arbitrary labels, such as decent and
indecent, moral and immoral, proper and improper,
pious and blasphemous. He was convinced that the
contradictions born of impulse and intuition often
discovered the eternal truths more readily than did
the positive demonstrations of logic and science.
His celebration of contradiction is at one with his
admonition against tutored guidance and expedient
dialectic, with his admonition against choosing
understanding over utterance, knowledge over life:

Let me have my own way,
Let others promulge the laws, I will make no account of
    the laws,
Let others praise eminent men and hold up peace, I hold
    up agitation and conflict,
  .   .   .   .   .
I give nothing as duties,
Where others give as duties I give as living impulses,
(Shall I give the heart's action as a duty?)
Let others dispose of questions, I dispose of nothing, I
    arouse unanswerable questions,
  .   .   .   .   .
I call to the world to distrust the accounts of my friends,
    but listen to my enemies, as I myself do,

41

I charge you forever reject those who would expound me,
    for I cannot expound myself,
I charge that there be no theory or school founded out
    of me,
I charge you leave all free, as I have left all free.
                "Myself and Mine," pp. 173-74

And his *Leaves* are defiantly strewn with contradictions. Whitman's most cherished dream, the
dream of a resplendent America effusing sweetness-
and-light and composed of a strong central government under which the individual would enjoy
absolute freedom, involved a contradiction not
even he could transcend except at his most visionary. Biographers, moreover, never leave off pointing out that Whitman's blustering unorthodoxy,
his chants of roistering rowdies and common prosti-
tutes, his raucous extroversion, his narcissism and
exhibitionism – all featured prominently in his
verse – are at variance with the man generally
remembered and reported as unobtrusive, gentle,
retiring, dreamy, soft-spoken, formal, and cautious-
ly reticent.

    Whitman and Nietzsche were not so remote in
either time or spirit from *Sturm und Drang* sentiments that they eschewed the guise of Promethean
Rebel. One will seek in vain, of course, if he pores
over their works for evidence of the gloomy egoist
or the romantic agony, though there are those who
would disagree. But the flamboyant image-smasher
is unmistakably present in both. For Nietzsche,
conscience meant the moral strength to oppose

whatever demeaned life, whatever was held sacred solely because it belonged to hoary tradition:

> The *ability* to contradict, the attainment of a *good* conscience in hostility to the accustomed, the traditional and the hallowed, – that is ... the step of all steps of the emancipated intellect.
>
> JOYFUL WISDOM, p. 232

Whitman and Nietzsche shared Hegel's view that contradiction, far from being a symptom of mental infirmity, was indicative of brilliance and creative insight. Their psychology of contradiction, like their psychology of good and evil, is also fundamentally Hegelian:

> According to Hegel the whole earth ... with its infinite variety, the past, the surroundings of today, or what may happen in the future, the contrarieties of material with spiritual, and of natural with artificial, are all, to the eye of the ensemblist, but necessary sides and unfoldings, different steps or links, in the endless process of creative thought, which, amid numberless apparent failures and contradictions, is held together by central and never-broken unity – not contradictions or failures at all, but radiations of one consistent and eternal purpose; the whole mass of everything steadily, unerringly tending and flowing toward the permanent *utile* and *morale*, as rivers to oceans. As life is the whole law and incessant effort of the visible universe, and death only the other or invisible side of the same, so the *utile*, so truth, so health, are the continuous-immutable laws of the moral universe, and vice and disease, with all their perturbations, are but transient, even if ever-so-prevalent expressions.
>
> SPECIMEN DAYS, pp. 236-37

43   Whitman and Nietzsche agreed with Hegel that

nothing is new under the sun; that no proposition (thesis) is ever fully and finally denied since every proposition contains something which eventually will give rise to a new proposition; that life and man's history comprise an infinite series of creative and destructive cataclysms evolving toward a superior humanity and culture. They also espoused the Heraclitean monism that repudiates the duality of spirit and matter, as well as the Heraclitean notion that the eternal flow, fomented and perpetuated by tensions and conflicts, is the permanent reality, the Being from which issues all becoming. Their contradiction of *status quo ante* and *status quo* was not nihilistic negation but an initial step to reinterpretation and reappraisal. They controverted in the spirit of enlightened optimists not in the spirit of despairing pessimists. In his autobiography, *Ecce Homo*, Nietzsche wrote: "I contradict as has never been contradicted before and am yet the opposite of a no-saying spirit." (Quoted by Walter Kaufmann, *Nietzsche: Philosopher Psychologist Antichrist*, New York, Meridian Press, 1956, p. 211.)

Whitman and Nietzsche believed that man is at one and the same time destroyer, preserver, and improver; that man's acceptance of the totality of life with its horrors and miseries, its evil as well as its good, was a necessary first step in his realization of a halcyon future when humanity would attain its highest expression and human ideals of love, beauty, and truth would be realized. In "Starting From Paumanok," Whitman argues that the whole justifies all of its parts; that the real poet's reci-

44

tatives must comprehend the harmony of the whole
in the very discord of its parts; and that nothing
which in the long run propels life forward, even
though it may arrest it temporarily, is maleficent:

> I make the poem of evil also, I commemorate that part
> also,
> I am myself just as much evil as good, and my nation is –
> and I say there is in fact no evil,
> (Or if there is I say it is just as important to you, to the
> land or to me, as any thing else.
>
> p. 18

These are the *ipsissima verba* of Nietzsche:

> *What* constitutes the value of those good and respected
> things, consists precisely in their being insidiously related,
> knotted, and crocheted to these evil and apparently op-
> posed things – perhaps even in being essentially identical
> with them.
>
> BEYOND GOOD AND EVIL, p. 214

Bacon's lie is Nietzsche's untruth, but for Nietzsche
its value is utilitarian (insofar as it furthers and
preserves life) as well as aesthetic:

> In reality the evil impulses are just in as high a degree
> expedient, indispensable, and conservative of the species
> as the good: – only their function is different.
>
> JOYFUL WISDOM, p. 40

However, it is not necessary to pore over their
works to surmise what Whitman and Nietzsche
would have taught regarding contradiction. The
devotee (not to mention the parodist) of the *Leaves*

45

can readily picture Whitman dialogizing on Brooklyn Bridge thus:

'I will effuse contradiction and show it underlying all. Whoever you are, to you endless contradictions! Was somebody asking dulcet consistency from me? I hasten to inform him or her I am the extoller of contradiction and conciliation. Whatever contradicts me exalts me, and whatever is contradicted by me is exalted. Did you think it was or could be otherwise?'

And, in the same way, the student of Nietzsche could readily conjure up a glowing vision of Zarathustra preaching as follows:

'O my friends, I teach you the word of words, the word of the Overman. It is the word contradiction. Do you hear it, my brothers? Revere it, cherish it. The logos of Zarathustra is contradiction. I teach you not veneration but desecration, not meek reception but heroic opposition, not peace but war, not servile conformity but heroic disagreement. There is more affirmation in the strong man's self-obeying than in all besotted consistency-mongers.'

Together with the pasquinades they penned against milksop diffidence, brash babbittry, and demeaning regimentation, they wrote earnestly on the need for testing anew the validity of mores, customs, and traditions. Like Socrates (whom Nietzsche specifically mentions in this connection) they urged the careful scrutiny of all beliefs commonly accepted as axiomatic and self-evident. To them, all systems as such were suspect. Consequently, they implored man to overhaul the moral laws and doctrines whose inviolability was the lie that enabled the unprincipled to batten upon the ingenuous. Before Whitman's Modern Man and Nietzsche's Overman could be brought forth, the way had to be paved not by good resolutions alone but by new realistic codes of behavior as well. The sacred task to which man must solemnly dedicate himself is characterized by Whitman in "Thou Mother With Thy Equal Brood" as follows:

Brain of the New World, what a task is thine,
To formulate the Modern – out of the peerless grandeur of
    the modern,
Out of thyself, comprising science, to recast poems,
    churches, art,
(Recast, maybe discard them, end them – maybe their
    work is done, who knows?)
By vision, hand, conception, on the background of the
    mighty past, the dead,
To limn with absolute faith the mighty living present.
                                                      p. 318

Jealous guardians of man's steadily-diminishing autonomy, Whitman and Nietzsche warned man to

47

pay no heed to the whisperings of the herd and to give his obedience only to the laws he formulated himself. They knew very well that the absence of external restraints did not insure freedom, and that the freedom to express one's thoughts is meaningless if one has no thoughts of his own to express. They reasoned that the man who cannot think for himself can command neither himself nor others and hence easily falls prey to the unscrupulous autocrat. To escape such debasing bondage and durance, they asked man to respect himself, to have faith in his own wisdom, to embrace earthly truths instead of illusory promises, to overcome his fears of social ostracism, to realize he cannot only because he will not, and to oppose with might and main whatever threatened the vital instinct. Then, partly out of a desire to enforce their lesson, partly because they appreciated the need for each age to reformulate the truths of knowledge, they taught their disciples the need for rejecting and superseding them, their own teachers.

In "By Blue Ontario's Shore," Whitman declares he is for those who have never been mastered, "for those whom laws, theories, conventions, can never master" (p. 250). In a three-line lyric, "To The States," he admonishes:

Resist, much, obey little,
Once unquestioning obedience, once fully enslaved.
p. 11

And, in "Song Of Myself," he foreshadows Nietzsche in beseeching man to become his own lawgiver

48

and the sole creator of all truth and of all values. After dismissing lecture-halls, books, and dogma as no better than beds of Procrustes, he cavalierly sweeps aside all self-doubts and self-doubters while voicing at the same time his faith in man's ability to know of himself through himself alone:

> You shall no longer take things at second or third hand, nor look through the eyes of the dead, nor feed on the spectres in books,
> You shall not look through my eyes either, nor take things from me,
> You shall listen to all sides and filter them from your self.
> He that by me spreads a wider breast than my own proves the width of my own,
> He most honors my style who learns under it to destroy the teacher.
>
> pp. 26; 65

Whitman and Nietzsche attributed many of man's ills to Philistinism and Pharisaism. They continually carped at man's reluctance to wean himself away from the misconceptions instilled into him in his youth and the expedient lies he devised to allay his anxieties. They pointed out that such misconceptions were generally the fabrications of neurotics who sought to impose upon the healthy the distorted perspectives of the ailing. And they inveighed against man's self-deceits because they represented a refusal to face reality and because they could alleviate the pain but could not extirpate the cause of man's despair. They traced many of man's compulsions, excesses, and aberrations to the unnatural repression imposed by rank superstitions, benighted mores, and arbitrary, unrealistic precepts

49

for social behavior. They perceptively noted that fear is at the root of all rational materialism, and cautioned against whatever reduces aspiration to a mirage and degrades the dreams of men into a mechanical destiny. Their attacks on traditional authorities, the past, and books were prompted by their convictions that one learns to live by living, not by reading or being told about life, that one only uses history in the service of the life that he has learned to live. Whatever man had not found to be true by his own experience was to be discarded. The atomic weights of all moral elements were to be ascertained anew.

Nietzsche's directives for effecting the above ends are identical with Whitman's. He, too, asks man to utilize "all his honesty, all his sturdiness and sincerity in his character, to help him to revolt against secondhand thought, secondhand learning, secondhand action" (*The Use & Abuse of History*, p. 72). He, too, scorned the blind devotee and the unquestioning disciple who mouthed the master's words with scant comprehension and no thought of testing their truth for himself:

"Be a man and do not follow me – but yourself! But yourself!"

JOYFUL WISDOM, p. 99

I now go away alone, my disciples! You too now go away and be alone! So I will have it.
Truly, I advise you: go away from me and guard yourselves against Zarathustra!...
One repays a teacher badly if one remains only a pupil.

ZARATHUSTRA, Hollingdale, p. 103

50

Nietzsche, too, saw in Socrates' incisive grilling the means of piercing through moral mendacities and exposing the hollowness of eternal as well as prevailing idols. Whitman, always an indefatigable stroller, always consumed by voracious curiosity, always in quest of disciples, always a sedulous self-diagnostician, never a hat-doffer nor fawner before the unproven great, naturally felt an affinity with the Athenian peripatetic:

I am he who walks the States with a barb'd tongue,
    questioning every one I meet,
Who are you that wanted only to be told what you knew
    before?
Who are you that wanted only a book to join in your
    nonsense?

BY BLUE ONTARIO'S SHORE, p. 242

And Nietzsche was equally impressed by Socrates' intrepid cross-examining which deflated and confounded so many pretenders to wisdom and virtue:

It seems to me more and more that the philosopher, being *necessarily* a man of tomorrow and the day after tomorrow, has at all times stood, and has *had* to stand, in opposition to his today. ... All these extraordinary furtherers of mankind ... have hitherto found their task, their hard, unwanted, peremptory task – but ultimately also the greatness of their task – in being the bad conscience of their time. ... At all times they showed how much hypocrisy, indolence, letting oneself go and letting oneself fall, how many lies, were hidden under the most respected type of their current morality...

BEYOND GOOD AND EVIL, pp. 135-36

51   To Zarathustra, the joyous wisdom is the awareness

that life's secret is accessible to man as soon as man discovers he can plumb it all alone. Nietzsche was convinced that nihilism, the *mal de siècle*, proceeded from the atrophy of will induced by a Christianity of self-mutilation and from the hypertrophy of reason induced by a purely theoretical empiricism. His un-holy crusade was launched in order to restore to man the freedom, self-respect, self-reliance, and courage which Christianity had neutralized and subverted. Nietzsche, however, could only give directions; each individual must himself liberate his individuality from the sty of the herd-animal and purge himself of morality's decoctions. Man must not turn for aid either to a God who was dead or to a science which was based more on prejudice than fact. He must walk alone and hearken only to the voice of his own oneness among the many. "He who obeys," Zarathustra instructs, *"does not listen to himself!"* (*Zarathustra*, Hollingdale, p. 218) And, in *Joyful Wisdom*, we read:

I don't want people to do anything *after* me; I want every one to do something *before* himself (as a pattern to himself) – just as *I* do.

pp. 206-7

Regardless, however, of how much they might entreat their adherents to supplant their preceptors, it was characteristic of Whitman and Nietzsche to rush after the mythical catechumens they had just dismissed with afterthoughts and a never-ceasing flow of additional precepts. Their solicitude and possessiveness is indeed touching when it is not comical. Both, moreover, reassure us that their

52

words will, in time, be scattered, like ashes and sparks from an unextinguished hearth, among mankind. They often put us in mind of Christ as they foretell the magic potency of their irresistible words:

I teach straying from me, yet who can stray from me?
I follow you whoever you are from the present hour,
My words itch at your ears till you understand them.
SONG OF MYSELF, p. 65

At the same time, they cautioned new recruits to their banners that their road was paved with the pulverized rubble of shattered tablets and shrines and littered with the debris of pale warriors. It was not a road for the faint of heart and mollycoddled. Lovers of security, respectability, and the bovine bliss of ignorance never set foot on it. Those who tramped a perpetual journey on this road did not slink by or creep along like lepers, mendicants, and lickspittles; they strolled along like lords of the earth, courting society's obloquy, inviting the screaks of Pecksniffian grimalkins. They were the first to grant that the stern realities they asked man to confront were hardly calculated to mitigate anxiety. Misgivings are not set at rest upon learning that respected truths are specious rationalizations, that cherished hopes are delusive phantoms, that responsibility is man's alone and viability the law of the cosmos.

Whitman admitted his draught was bitter but insisted that whoever wished to learn his lesson complete must be prepared to quaff his Socratic hemlock without demur:

53

I know my words are weapons full of danger, full of death,
For I confront peace, security, and all settled laws, to
    unsettle them,
I am more resolute because all have denied me ...
I heed not ... cautions, majorities, nor ridicule,
And the threat of ... hell is little or nothing to me,
And the lure of ... heaven is little or nothing to me.
AS I LAY WITH MY HEAD IN YOUR LAP CAMERADO, p. 229

No less exacting, Nietzsche requires hardihood and
self-mastery of those who would follow him. His
roses can be plucked only at the risk of painful
thornpricks and bleeding fingers. His companions
are culled mainly from those constipated by herd
prescriptives. They and they alone are worthy of
the Promethean task of creating all the truth and
all the values that can have any meaning for man:

Creation – that is the great redemption from suffering,
and life's easement. But that the creator may exist, that
itself requires suffering and much transformation.
Yes, there must be much bitter dying in your life, you
creators! Thus you are advocates and justifiers of all
transitoriness.

ZARATHUSTRA, Hollingdale, p. 111

He lauds Socratic humility but scorns cloistered
virtue. He echoes Blake's insight that convictions
are prisons:

One should not be deceived: great spirits are skeptics.
Zarathustra is a skeptic. Strength, *freedom* which is born
of the strength and overstrength of the spirit, proves
itself by skepticism. Men of conviction are not worthy of
the least consideration in fundamental questions of value
and disvalue. Convictions are prisons.

THE ANTICHRIST, PORTABLE NIETZSCHE, p. 638

54

The readers Nietzsche desires for himself are such as laugh at ostracism. They covet truths as truths rather than as aids to material advantage. They are not afraid to pose questions which jeopardize their security and very lives. They understand Nietzsche's intent is not to pour new wine but to destroy casks and empty bottles whose contents have soured and, simultaneously, to bring up rare vintages from cellars whose stocks have been forgotten or buried under ruins in the course of centuries. They share Nietzsche's contentions that prevailing piety is impious, that prevailing veracity is mendacious, that prevailing goodness is wickedness. They appreciate Nietzsche's psychological insight that conformity to the law breeds corruption and depravity in the ranks of the weak and dependent. And they comprehend that, since Nietzsche's revaluation is a perspicacious scrutiny, reassessment, and rearrangement of existing verities, it is basically an affirmation (and not nihilism) even though it is arrived at only after the honest recognition and negation of all found to be no longer true, vital, and conducive to the growth of human greatness. It is of them that Nietzsche speaks when he says:

We ourselves, we free spirits, are nothing less than a "revaluation of all values," an *incarnate* declaration of war and triumph over all ancient conceptions of "true" and "untrue."

THE ANTICHRIST, PORTABLE NIETZSCHE, p. 579

Whitman's and Nietzsche's passionate embrace of life in its totality – in its glowing plenitude and in its guttering twilight, in its pleasures and in its pains, in its ecstatic joys and in its hideous horrors – is enunciated frequently and eloquently in most of their major works. It is closely associated with their pagan paeans hymning man's body and senses, with their view of death as a phase in life's cycle rather than the terminus of life, with their conviction that man is master of his fate and can extricate himself from the quagmire of doubt and fear by his own unaided exertions.

Their championing of intuition was occasioned partly by their personal experience regarding its efficacy and partly by the derision with which scientific rationalists dismissed it. Similarly, their stout defense of man's instincts and bodily passions was motivated partly by their indignant rejection of the traditional doctrine that held spirit and matter were separate and distinct, and partly by their impatience with the false prudery and blind stupidity that refused to acknowledge the elementary facts of life. Their deification of the senses and impulses was neither hedonism nor primitivism; it was principally a naturalistic repudiation of the division between flesh and spirit. Like Blake and Goethe, they held sacrosanct the impulse to life which pervades all animate objects. They also shared Blake's view that virtue and vice could be understood only in terms of innocence and experience, and that lamb and tiger were to be blessed alike since their opposition provided both the basis

56

of life and also the tension which advanced life. To them, the Edenic Myth was an embodiment of life's dialectic where the State of Innocence was the thesis, the Transgression represented the antithesis, and Man's Fate signified the synthesis. In addition, both Whitman and Nietzsche followed Blake's lead and anticipated Freud by speaking out forthrightly against the unnatural repression of desires. Both, moreover, located the forces that suppressed the free exercise of man's creative and procreative energies in the Church and in Convention. Whitman viewed the human body as a holy temple every ounce as divine as any church edifice, and his wrath knew no bounds when belaboring those who found any part of it unclean or degrading. He was at one with Blake in believing that the body is that part of the soul which we cannot see, and consequently felt that ascetic mortification or religious denigration of the body was a sin against life. Nietzsche contended that the Church was the State's ally in imposing a uniformity of mediocrity that was death to virtually all creative endeavor. And he predicted the inhuman outrages of Prussianism and the Nazis by the simple logic of asking what was the inevitable consequence of the flagellation theology of Luther which told men they were totally depraved by nature and then excoriated them for being what they inescapably were.

As Poet of the Body and singer of man's glorious sentiency, Whitman joins Blake in finding the genitals beautiful, in extolling touch as a touchstone to eternity, in affirming all conceptions though maculate are holy, and in understanding most puritanism to be indicative of the weakness of desire:

Copulation is no more rank to me than death is.
I believe in the flesh and the appetites.
On women fit for conception I start bigger and nimbler
    babes.
If any thing is sacred the human body is sacred.

pp. 42; 57; 75

As the chanter of Adamic songs, as the one aching with amorous love, as the primordial seed-bearer, with the potent original loins, as a super-American Zeus, Whitman undertakes to father the noble future generations of the States by impregnating American womanhood:

It is I, you women, I make my way,
I am stern, acrid, large, undissuadable, but I love you,
I do not hurt you any more than is necessary for you,
I pour the stuff to start sons and daughters fit for these
    States.

A WOMAN WAITS FOR ME, p. 77

He calls neither for promiscuity nor for bacchanalia. He does not minimize the ecstasy of sexual congress but he makes it clear that he prizes it chiefly as a means of perpetuating a perfectible humanity he fervently hopes will commence its evolution towards perfection in the immediate future. Though an egalitarian and, like Christ, one who would not turn away from the lowly prostitute, Whitman shared Nietzsche's point of view in seeing woman's role as primarily that of a mother. Nietzsche's view of women was for the most part Miltonic, but he is

58

every inch as impassioned as Whitman in scourging
the hair-shirted despisers of the body, and in de-
crying those who resort to sex as to a drug:

Sex: for free hearts, innocent and free, the garden happiness of the earth, the future's exuberant gratitude to the
present.
Sex: only for the wilted, a sweet poison; for the lion-
willed, however, the great invigoration of the heart and
the reverently reserved wine of wines.
Sex: the happiness that is the great parable of a higher
happiness and the highest hope.

ZARATHUSTRA, p. 300

Nietzsche did not exclude the ascetic from his types
of the great man which included the artist and the
philosopher. But there seems little doubt that his
highest commendation was reserved for the passionate being who was perfect master of his passions. Nietzsche was very Aristotelian in deeming
both the man who acted on blind impulse and also
the man who forcibly thwarted his desires vastly
inferior to the man who rationally controlled his
instincts. He admired Socrates for recognizing
Athenian decadence was the consequence of man's
appetites running amuck. But he deplored Socrates'
drastic cure which called for rationality at any
price. His attitude toward the passions, his theory
of sublimation, and the basis for his attacks against
Christianity are all made explicitly clear in the
following passage from *Twilight of the Idols:*

All passions have a phase when they are merely disastrous,
when they drag down their victim with the weight of
stupidity – and a later, very much later phase when they

59

wed the spirit, when they "spiritualize" themselves. Formerly, in view of the element of stupidity in passion, war was declared on passion itself, its destruction was plotted; all the old moral monsters are agreed on this: *il faut tuer les passions*. The most famous formula for this is to be found in the New Testament, in that Sermon on the Mount, where, incidentally, things are by no means looked at from a height. There it is said, for example, with particular reference to sexuality: "If thy eye offend thee, pluck it out." Fortunately, no Christian acts in accordance with this precept. *Destroying* the passions and cravings, merely as a preventive measure against their stupidity and the unpleasant consequences of this stupidity – today this itself strikes us as merely another acute form of stupidity. We no longer admire dentists who "pluck out" teeth so that they will not hurt any more.

To be fair, it should be admitted, however, that on the ground out of which Christianity grew, the concept of the "*spiritualization* of passion" could never have been formed. After all the first church, as is well known, fought *against* the "intelligent" in favor of the "poor in spirit." How could one expect from it an intelligent war against passion? The church fights passion with excision in every sense: its practice, its "cure," is *castratism*. It never asks: "How can one spiritualize, beautify, deify a craving?" It has at all times laid the stress of discipline on extirpation (of sensuality, of pride, of the lust to rule, of avarice, of vengefulness). But an attack on the roots of passion means an attack on the roots of life: the practice of the church is *hostile to life*.

PORTABLE NIETZSCHE, pp. 486-87

Nietzsche realized the sexual urge could easily degenerate into mere concupiscence but he was certain that just as man can rise above animality so can man's libido be refined. He persistently pointed out that in Greece sex was viewed as a sign of

health and that it was only with Christianity's
advent that it came to be seen as a bugbear:

I know no higher symbolism than this *Greek* symbolism of
the Dionysian festivals. Here the most profound instinct
of life, that directed toward the future of life, the enternity
of life, is experienced religiously – and the way to life,
procreation, as the *holy* way. It was Christianity, with its
ressentiment against life at the bottom of its heart, which
first made something unclean of sexuality: it threw *filth* on
the origin, on the presupposition of our life.
TWILIGHT OF THE IDOLS, PORTABLE NIETZSCHE, p. 562

For Nietzsche, as for Whitman, the arch foes of life
were the dry-as-dust scholars and preachers. Both
assailed the fallacy which conferred on reason the
principal role in the apperception of external reality. Their quarrel, of course, was not with reason
per se but rather with the scientism which relegated
the testimony of the senses and the intuition to the
realm of superstition. They both hated absolute
empiricisms and desiccated scholasticisms.

Knowledge educed from cerebral synthesis cannot
by itself satisfy man's burgeoning curiosity. Life's
totality cannot be apprehended by ratiocinative
schematizations alone. Analysis, by its very nature,
is inimical to life; beyond a certain point, the
breakdown of many of life's hypostatic simples may
be attended with fatal consequences. In "When I
Heard The Learn'd Astronomer," Whitman avers
that truth cannot be arrived at by syllogizing; it
must be felt like an impulse from a vernal wood.
In "Song Of Myself," he bestows the first prize
upon the scientists. At the same time, however, he

61

asserts that, although their facts are useful, facts are not his personal lares. And, later in the same poem, he is appreciably less conciliatory toward pedagogues:

All truths wait in all things,
They neither hasten their own delivery nor resist it,
They do not need the obstetric forceps of the surgeon,
.   .   .
Logic and sermons never convince,
The damp of the night drives deeper into my soul.

p. 46

Whitman was at one with Emerson and Nietzsche in believing that history, books, and book-learning were not to be worshipped as deities but used as tools. Too many books and histories are written by bookworms who are not original thinkers and who commence their writing with preconceived notions and with traditional as well as current prejudices. Hence books and dogmatic pedagogues may do more harm than good by stifling the individual's inclination for independent thought, by dulling his capacity for original observation, and by instilling in him not only false or obsolete information but also a predisposition to their own bias. Whitman echoed Emerson in asserting the active soul is an infinitely surer guide to wisdom than any book or lecturer:

Wisdom is not finally tested in schools,
Wisdom cannot be pass'd from one having it to another
    not having it,
Wisdom is of the soul, is not susceptible of proof, is its
    own proof.

SONG OF THE OPEN ROAD, p. 110

62

The most a good teacher could hope or wish to do would be to stimulate and inspire his pupils to cogitate on their own. No education can be valid or complete, moreover, which does not offer the student the opportunity to test his theoretical learning in the open air on life's broad highway. Only by setting out with Whitman on a marathon hike can the student check out the truths he was taught and master the eternal verities of the earth:

Allons! whoever you are come travel with me!
Traveling with me you find what never tires.
The earth never tires,
The earth is rude, silent, incomprehensible at first, Nature
    is rude and incomprehensible at first,
Be not discouraged, keep on, there are divine things well
    envelop'd,
I swear to you there are divine things more beautiful than
    words can tell.
                        SONG OF THE OPEN ROAD, p. 111

One impulse from his own heart or that of his teacher could teach the student more of man, of moral evil and of good, than all the sages. Whitman concurred with Blake that "Demonstration is only by bodily Senses":

(I and mine do not convince by arguments, similes,
    rhymes,
We convince by our presence.)
                        SONG OF THE OPEN ROAD, p. 112

Oxen that rattle the yoke and chain or halt in the leafy
    shade, what is that you express in your eyes?
It seems to me more than all the print I have read in
    my life.

63   SONG OF MYSELF, p. 33

Nietzsche's thinking adheres closely to Whitman's on this subject. He, too, proclaimed the "innocence of the senses" (*Zarathustra*, p. 166); he, too, remarked that "in the end, one experiences only oneself" (*Zarathustra*, p. 264). Nietzsche, too, voiced grave doubts in regard to scholastic panjandrums:

> Beware of the scholars! They hate you, for they are sterile. ... Such men boast they do not lie: but the inability to lie is far from the love of truth.
>
> ZARATHUSTRA, p. 402

The German philosopher had nothing but contempt for those who with the baedekers of astigmatic pedants clutched tightly in their hands peered at life through scientific blinders. He had not read Blake and Whitman but he recalled Goethe's sentiments that it is the judgment, and not the senses, which is usually at fault in human errors of perception:

> The senses ... do not lie at all. What we *make* of their testimony, that alone introduces lies. ... "Reason" is the cause of our falsification of the testimony of the senses.
>
> TWILIGHT OF THE IDOLS, PORTABLE NIETZSCHE, pp. 480-81

As already indicated, both Whitman and Nietzsche belligerently defended the senses and the body against the perennial grumbling of the excessively modest. Whitman is the rhapsodist of the body as much as he is the rhapsodist of the soul. He maintains that the two are, in fact, one and indivisible; that all that is soul and all that is not soul is equally precious:

64

Strange and hard the paradox true I give,
Objects gross and the unseen soul are one.
A SONG FOR OCCUPATIONS, p. 158

Clear and sweet is my soul, and clear and sweet is all that
    is not my soul.
Lack one lacks both, and the unseen is proved by the seen,
Till that becomes unseen and receives proof in its turn.

I believe in you my soul, the other I am must not abase
    itself to you,
And you must not be abased to the other.
SONG OF MYSELF, pp. 26; 27

COME, SAID MY SOUL,
SUCH VERSES FOR MY BODY LET US WRITE, (FOR WE ARE
ONE.)
motto for LEAVES OF GRASS, p. 3

Elsewhere, however, he appears to adhere to the orthodox notion that the soul is the immortal portion of man and the body is the mortal portion subject to decay and decomposition – even though the dead body is admirable fertilizer and hence breeds of new life and enjoys a kind of phoenix-like eternity:

I depart as air, I shake my white locks at the runaway sun,
I effuse my flesh in eddies, and drift it in lacy jags.

I bequeath myself to the dirt to grow from the grass I love,
If you want me again look for me under your boot-soles.
SONG OF MYSELF, p. 68

Behold this compost! behold it well!
Perhaps every mite has once form'd part of a sick person –
    yet behold!
The grass of spring covers the prairies,

The summer growth is innocent and disdainful above all
those strata of sour dead.
AUTUMN RIVULETS, p. 261

And I have dream'd that the purpose and essence of the
known life, the transient,
Is to form and decide identity for the unknown life, the
permanent.

If all came but to ashes of dung,
If maggots and rats ended us, then Alarum! for we are
betray'd,
Then indeed suspicion of death.
TO THINK OF TIME, p. 307

Actually, there is no contradiction since Whitman
was quite Platonic (indirectly through Emerson
and Carlyle) in believing that ultimate reality was
spiritual. He held that every evanescent, material
object had its permanent, spiritual counterpart
which he generally referred to as its eidolon. All
objects, in other words, were palpable models,
visible replicas, tangible manifestations, tellurian
configurations of their corresponding archetypes.
Nothing is lost in the universe. All objects, after a
spell of mortality, enjoy everlasting life. But mortality is not thereby less estimable. The mortal
shell, which is shed at death, is, during life, inextricably linked to its immortal part. What is
more, Whitman's orientation was too sensorial and
his leaning toward philosophical sensationalism too
pronounced to admit of his prizing the reality after
the grave more than the reality of his beloved grass.
His huzzas are apportioned equally among Paumanok's sandy beaches and eternity's vast deserts: 66

I will make the poems of materials, for I think they are to
    be the most spiritual poems,
And I will make the poems of my body and of mortality,
For I think I shall then supply myself with the poems of
    my soul and of immortality.

Was somebody asking to see the soul?
See, your own shape and countenance, persons, substances,
    beasts, the trees, the running rivers, the rocks and
    sands.

All hold spiritual joys and afterwards loosen them;
How can the real body ever die and be buried?
Of your real body and any man's or woman's real body,
Item for item it will elude the hands of the corpse-cleaners
    and pass to fitting spheres,
Carrying what has accrued to it from the moment of birth
    to the moment of death.

    .   .   .

Behold, the body includes and is the meaning, the main
    concern, and includes and is the soul;
Whoever you are, how superb and how divine is your
    body, or any part of it!
           STARTING FROM PAUMANOK, pp. 17; 20-21

I believe of all those men and women that fill'd the un-
    named lands, every one exists this hour here or else-
    where, invisible to us,
In exact proportion to what he or she grew from in life,
    and out of what he or she did, felt, became, loved,
    sinn'd, in life.

    .   .   .

I suspect their results curiously await in the yet unseen
    world, counterparts of what accrued to them in the
    seen world.
           UNNAMED LANDS, p. 264

67   Nietzsche wholeheartedly agreed with Whitman

that the duality of impulse (passion) and reason (spirit) was utter nonsense:

The pure spirit is the pure lie.

The "pure spirit" is a pure stupidity: if we subtract the nervous system and the senses – the "mortal shroud" – *then we miscalculate* – that is all!
THE ANTICHRIST, PORTABLE NIETZSCHE, pp. 575; 581

But Nietzsche, of course, was wholly naturalistic. He disbelieved all speculations relating to an afterlife. He never glimpsed any transcendent destiny hovering in the wings poised to bring salvation to man, the poor player strutting and fretting his brief hour upon life's stage. Identity beyond the grave was to Nietzsche a preposterous absurdity and concepts such as Platonic Ideas and an immortal soul he regarded as perversely asinine. For Nietzsche, moreover, the real was what was demonstrably existent. What he found detestable in Christianity was its atrocious misrepresentations of actuality, its distempered fabrications, and its ingrained dissimulation. In Christianity, Nietzsche discovered not only the irrationality of the insane but also the decadence of a hireling society and the nihilism of craven cowardice:

In Christianity neither morality nor religion has even a single point of contact with reality. ... This *world of pure fiction* is vastly inferior to the world of dreams insofar as the latter *mirrors* reality, whereas the former falsifies, devalues, and negates reality. Once the concept of "nature" had been invented as the opposite of "God," "natural" had to become a synonym of "reprehensible":

68

this whole world of fiction is rooted in *hatred* of the natural (of reality!); it is the expression of a profound vexation at the sight of reality.

THE ANTICHRIST, PORTABLE NIETZSCHE, pp. 581-582

Nietzsche shared Whitman's distrust of theoreticians whose ponderous tomes replete with involved abstractions were totally divorced from the vocation of living and consequently hostile to life itself. But, cheek by jowl, with Whitman, the anti-metaphysician, we find Whitman, the supreme metaphysician; whereas, in Nietzsche, the obstinate refusal of all supernatural consolation assumes the proportions of zealotry. Whitman was as existential as Nietzsche in prizing the growth of the human personality above everything else, but, like the Tennyson of *In Memoriam*, he felt "earth is darkness at the core and dust and ashes all that is" if one cannot believe in personal immortality. Nietzsche, on the other hand, although he, too, eventually embraced a semi-mystical concept, that of the eternal recurrence, devoted much of his writing to finding the means of avoiding futilitarian despair while learning to live without God, the hope of heaven, and the promise of salvation. It is also important to note that, although Whitman would qualify for inclusion in a list of anti-rationalists that would include Emerson, Blake, and D. H. Lawrence, Nietzsche would not. In Whitman, the basic urge is creative (which subsumes the sexual urge); hence, for Whitman, the passions enjoy as much prestige as the rational faculties. What is more, since Whitman agrees with Emerson that

69

human impulses are divinely-inspired, it is obvious
that such impulses have little if any need of reason's
husbandry. Nietzsche's position is by no means
identical. He is not a rationalist since he does not
concede that reason is the principal motive power
in man. But neither is he an anti-rationalist. In
Nietzsche, the basic urge is the will-to-power; and
the rational faculty and the passions are both
expressions in different guises of this urge. Furthermore, as already indicated, the man most highly
esteemed by Nietzsche is the man who overcomes
himself, who achieves a rational mastery over his
passions.

Yet, insofar as priests enjoined the excision
rather than rarefaction of the instincts, Nietzsche
was even more ready than Whitman to pillory
them. At times, both displayed tolerance and
sympathy. With his characteristic aplomb, Whitman, in *Song of Myself*, expansively assures priests
he does not particularly detest them: "I do not
despise you priests, all time, the world over" (p. 60).
And Zarathustra confides to his pupils that he is
"moved by compassion for these priests" (*Zarathustra*, p. 203). It was not, however, in either of
their natures to refrain for long from twitting the
dispensers of supernal caudle and the hawkers of
quack catholicons. Inasmuch as priests are leagued
with Urizens in belittling the senses, in necrosing
life, in weaving webs of sin, Whitman feels it is
time to end their reign. Whatever useful functions
they may have performed in the past can now be
better carried out by the poets:

70

Allons! from all formules!
From your formules, O bat-eyed and materialistic priests.
There will shortly be no more priests, I say their work is
   done.
SONG OF THE OPEN ROAD, p. 112; BY BLUE ONTARIO'S
   SHORE, p. 248

"The mumbling and screaming priest" is "soon deserted" (*Thoughts*, p. 333) and is succeeded by the poet singing the organic unity of all being, praising the body as the privileged place of joy, arousing each individual to partake of the delicious plenitude of earth's bounty. Nietzsche's epithets are equally pungent and graphic. His verbal artillery barrage against the tonsured servants of the church rakes them for inveighing against the attitude of here or nowhere, for disvaluing reason to enshrine faith, and for sowing the seeds of an invidious *ressentiment*. To Nietzsche, the priest is the deformed Thersites, mocking what he has not the courage or capacity to enjoy, maliciously maligning, because he envies, whatever is strong, healthy, and vitally beautiful:

As long as the priest was considered the supreme type, *every* valuable kind of human being was devaluated. The time will come, I promise, when the priest will be considered the lowest type, our Chandala, the most mendacious, the most indecent kind of human being.
   TWILIGHT OF THE IDOLS, PORTABLE NIETZSCHE, p. 550

Nietzsche was nettled also by the theologians' nihilism which found the human body to be a cesspool of corruption, which disclaimed human efforts

towards betterment, and which disdained all truths
except the dogmata of the church:

> As long as the priest is considered a *higher* type of man –
> this *professional* negator, slanderer, and poisoner of life –
> there is no answer to the question: what *is* truth? For
> truth has been stood on its head when the conscious
> advocate of nothingness and negation is accepted as the
> representative of "truth."
>
> THE ANTICHRIST, PORTABLE NIETZSCHE, p. 575

But what Nietzsche found most hateful of all was
that the priests' untruths and myths were employed to serve personal ambition, to enable them to
become masters over a cowed and insecure congre-
gation:

> All the concepts of the church have been recognized for
> what they are, the most malignant counterfeits that exist,
> the aim of which is to devalue nature and natural values;
> the priest himself has been recognized for what he is, the
> most dangerous kind of parasite, the real poison-spider
> of life.
>
> THE ANTICHRIST, PORTABLE NIETZSCHE, p. 611

Whitman anticipated many of Nietzsche's stric-
tures against religion, but, although he carried
many of these further than Emerson would have
dared, he generally stopped short of Nietzsche's
relentless and often hysterical conclusions. In addition, Whitman's omnivorousness led him many
times to entertain two or more opposed notions
simultaneously. A Quaker by birth and strongly
mindful of Emerson's thought, Whitman deemed
man perfectly capable of understanding God and
God's ways without benefit of clergy and church.   72

He believed a new religion was both inevitable and desirable. He predicted that the priest would be replaced by the bard whose function would be to arouse the individual's awareness of the divine afflatus in himself, in others, and in all nature. Thus Whitman, like Nietzsche, was a severe critic of orthodox Christianity and its products. But Whitman's criticism lacks Nietzsche's frenzied mordacity. However much Whitman might regret that Christian doctrine was mostly a hideous travesty of Christ's teachings, however much his hatred might be quickened against the ruthless profiteering which was Christian piety and at the vicious exploitation which was Christian love, he, nevertheless, does not dispense with divinity and the divine principle. The supernatural might not be of more moment than the natural, but Whitman did not, therefore, reject the former. If man was as divine as anything, it was because he carried divinity within him, because he shared with all creation a portion of the divine cosmic substance that was both the source and the destination of all life. But Whitman does approach Nietzsche's position that, since gods are man's creations, man should worship only himself. After nonchalantly reciting the roll call of past deities, Whitman elbows them aside as circumspect vendors of metaphysical palliatives. He grants their historical existence but is not overawed by them. He acknowledges they served their times and aided man in his tender infancy. Now, however, that man has matured, he should sing in his own voice and fly with his own pinions. The old

gods were forerunners, not the ultimate deities.
Whitman studies them only to surpass them, only
in order to become himself a superior creator. The
truths vouchsafed by special revelations may do
well; but the truths disclosed by one's self do
equally well if not better:

Magnifying and applying come I,
Outbidding at the start the old cautious hucksters,
Taking myself the exact dimensions of Jehovah,
Lithographing Kronos, Zeus his son, and Hercules his
    grandson,
Buying drafts of Osiris, Isis, Belus, Brahma, Buddha,
     .   .   .

Taking them all for what they are and not a cent more,
Admitting they were alive and did the work of their days,
(They bore mites as for unfledg'd birds who have now to
    rise and fly and sing for themselves.)
     .   .   .

Not objecting to special revelations, considering a curl of
    smoke or a hair on the back of my hand just as
    curious as any revelation,
     .   .   .

The supernatural of no account, myself waiting my time
    to be one of the supremes, ...
By my life-lumps! becoming already a creator.
                      SONG OF MYSELF, pp. 58-59

Nietzsche picks up the argument where Whitman
leaves off. He hammers away at the imperative
need for subordinating man's creations to man. He
warns against adoring that which enjoys sanctity
solely by man's permission. He cautions that the
nature of illusion is not to recognize itself as such,
but to consider itself true: the clay figure shaped
by frolicking children may, in time, its origins long
since obscured, be revered as a deity by those who

74

attribute to it qualities it never had. Nietzsche might have admired the daring and drive of Conrad's Kurtz; but the natives' idolatry of his person to which Kurtz cynically consented would have revolted the German philosopher who sired the Superman. Probably more congenial to Nietzsche would be the custom followed in the utopian realm Aldous Huxley describes in his novel, *Island*. In Pala, the island utopia, scarecrows are dolls made to resemble gods in order "to make the children understand that all gods are homemade, and that it's we who pull their strings and so give them the power to pull us" (p. 234). Zarathustra never leaves off preaching that superterrestrial felicities are the poppy and mandragora of human vampires and leeches whose inveterate distrust of life precludes clear sight and realistic thought. Gods he considers the hectic hallucinations of psychotic fantasts whose longing for another and better life testifies to their maladjustment. On one occasion, he summons the faithful, like a muezzin from a minaret, to hear his confession: he, too, was once an arrant afterworldsman who thought the world and its inhabitants the work of a suffering and unhappy God. Very soon, however, he came to his senses:

> Once Zarathustra too cast his deluded fancy beyond mankind, like all afterworldsmen. Then the world seemed to me the work of a suffering and tormented God.
>
> .   .   .
>
> Ah, brothers, this God which I created was human work and human madness, like all gods!

He was human, and only a poor piece of man and Ego:
this phantom came to me from my own fire and ashes,
that is the truth! It did not come to me from the 'beyond'!
ZARATHUSTRA, Hollingdale, pp. 58-59

And possibly with a backward glance at Kierkegaard Zarathustra concludes:

Weariness, which wants to reach the ultimate with a
single leap, with a death-leap, a poor ignorant weariness,
which no longer wants even to want: that created all gods
and afterworlds.
ZARATHUSTRA, Hollingdale, p. 59

This belief, that creation was a human prerogative,
also figures in Nietzsche's interpretation of art and
Greek tragedy. According to Nietzsche, art served
the Greeks as morality (ethics) served Socrates and
Christianity: it was the means by which horrid
reality was converted into pleasure, the means by
which life triumphed over death, the means by
which man gained a victory over the intolerable
pain of existence. Whereas Christianity led its followers to flee and hate life, art enabled the Greek
to view life as an enjoyable game. Nietzsche attributed to the Greeks the knowledge that life can
best be understood and justified as an aesthetic
phenomenon. He held that Attic tragedy was the
result of a happy marriage between Apollonian
art and Dionysian art. Apollonian art taught the
Greeks to incorporate into plastic representations
the whole of phenomenal reality including its
grisliest horrors; by translating the ghastliest of
terrors to the eternal realm of artifact – outside of

76

life, beyond pain, free of contingency and mutability – Apollonian art bestowed upon them just that shade of unreality which permitted the beholder to gaze upon them without being turned to stone. In this way, the Greeks could enjoy as spectacle the beauty of the most forbidding abominations. Dionysian art taught the Greeks how to transcend reality through an ecstatic rapture which made them one with the primal, creative urge of the cosmos; Dionysian art enabled them to lose and rediscover their individual selves in the universal identity of all things. Attic tragedy taught the Athenian the identity of spectacle and spectator; man is at once creator, actor, and spectator for he not only engenders the suffering he endures, but, by virtue of being able to contemplate it, he is also able to justify it and life as well. In other words, once he is made aware of his identity with all things, man finds the beauty of life's drama adequate compensation for the suffering he endures as an actor of the representation. The controlled tension achieved by Attic tragedy in harmoniously fusing rational and irrational, intelligence and passion, knowledge and instinct, form and content, was highly admired by Nietzsche. We have seen that he esteemed the man who was able to overcome himself, who was able to mold his inchoate creative energies into constructive, coherent thought or literature, who was able to sublimate his instinctual drives into art or spirituality, who was able to blend compatibly the Apollonian and Dionysian. This is the man whom Nietzsche variously desig-

77

nated as the knower, the creator, the Superman. He is above all the man who is aware of himself as the one and only creator:

> Prometheus had first to *fancy* that he had *stolen* the light, and that he did penance for the theft, – in order finally to discover that he had created the light, *in that he had longed* for the light, and that not only man, but also *God*, had been the work of *his* hands and the clay in his hands. All mere creations of the Creator!
>
> JOYFUL WISDOM, p. 234

It was precisely such an awareness, Nietzsche was convinced, that made it possible for the Greek, with his superabundant vitality and his art, not only to confront a world ruled by Chance and Maya, but also to affirm with gladness a life which a less vital race would have cursed for its cruelty and injustice. It was precisely this awareness which deterred the Greek from despairing at life's absurdity and stimulated him to reject the *odium fati* of passive nihilism and accept the *amor fati* of active nihilism. And, of course, it was precisely this awareness which was at the bottom of the whole of Nietzsche's philosophy.

The feeling of identity with all things in the universe, which Nietzsche held was experienced at the height of Dionysian rapture, was experienced by Whitman daily. We have shown that Whitman still adhered to the concepts of the soul's immortality and of God's existence. At the same time, Whitman remembered that at the end of *Nature*, Emerson had spoken of the self's capacity for divine creativity and that, in his essay on the

78

Oversoul, Emerson had said that "the simplest person who in his integrity worships God, becomes God." Whitman, therefore, was not at all reluctant to promulge that "nothing, not God, is greater than one's self is" (*Song of Myself*, p. 66); and that no "gods can exceed these that clasp me by the hand" (*Crossing Brooklyn Ferry*, p. 119). Whitman would in all likelihood have refused to preach with Zarathustra that "precisely this is godlike that there are gods, but no God!" (*Zarathustra, Hollingdale*, p. 220). He may even have strongly resented Zarathustra's statement to his followers that only since God "has lain in the grave have you again been resurrected" (*Zarathustra, Hollingdale*, p. 297). But it is very probable he would have assented to Zarathustra's words when the sage said:

> My Ego taught me a new pride, I teach it to men: No longer to bury the head in the sand of heavenly things, but to carry it freely, an earthly head which creates meaning for the earth! I teach mankind a new will: to desire this path that men have followed blindly, and to call it good and no more to creep aside from it, like the sick and dying!
>
> ZARATHUSTRA, Hollingdale, p. 60

Another key idea that confirmed Whitman and Nietzsche in their unconditional acceptance of existence was their recognition that death did not nullify and demean this world and this life, that death did not render this mortal and limited world less preferable than another. Whitman and Nietzsche opposed those slanderers of life who contended death validated their slander. They did not see death as an omnipotent sadist who frustrated man's hopes, mocked man's achievements, and disturbed man's sleep. Far from underscoring life's absurdity Whitman and Nietzsche believed death gave full meaning to life. They asked man to perceive and love death as an expression of life itself. It seemed to them that death's inevitability made life's joys doubly joyful; death's unfailing punctuality made explicit values that otherwise might have remained implicit only. Awareness of its periodic arrest in its biotic cycle, induces life to muster and deploy its forces with rare skill, and, by being thus roused to total self-awareness, to proclaim that it is the only value. Death stands somewhat in the same relation to life that knowledge does. Distrust of knowledge springs from the consciousness that knowledge is life's antithesis since knowledge dispels the chimera needed for life's preservation. Yet, at the same time, knowledge protects and promotes life since it compels man to refurbish the old, or devise new chimeras. Whitman and Nietzsche held that, in similar fashion, although death ostensibly negates life by calling attention to mortality, it can also be said to foster and reaffirm life. Death generates hopes and fears such as those taught by Christianity. Invariably, Hyperboreans, like Nietzsche, rebel against such hopes and fears. And, invariably, such rebellion, which has the courage for that which can really be known, eventuates in a renewed dedication to life and in the choice of Ithaca over Ogygia. Thus, *Timor Mortis Conturbat Me* is transmuted into "And I will show that nothing can

80

happen more beautiful than death" (*Starting From Paumanok*, p. 21). Whitman and Nietzsche chronicled death not in ululant threnodies but in valedictions forbidding mourning.

As long as there is the minutest spark of life, Whitman contends, death's conquests prove spurious. Every lover's morrow laughs to scorn death's vaunted dominion. Every act of creation triumphs over death everlastingly. Every germination diminishes death. Every birth is a victory over death:

> The smallest sprout shows there is really no death,
> And if ever there was it led forward life, and does not
>   wait at the end to arrest it,
> And ceas'd the moment life appear'd.
>
> SONG OF MYSELF, p. 29

It is worth noting that Whitman once planned a series of poems which, like *Passage to India*, would celebrate the life after death, and thus would serve both as complement and counterpart to *Leaves of Grass*. That he never did does not signify he entertained doubts about invisible reality. Several poems suggest the contrary. What it does indicate is that the poet realized his emphasis was on the visible and knowable and that he was content to let it remain so. It also explains why, as often as not, death is treated within the context of this world rather than the context of the other world. As remarked hereinbefore, Whitman shared Nietzsche's opinion that what man required was a philosophy of living, not a philosophy of salvation. For such a philosophy, death-in-life is more important than life-in-death. From what Thoreau

81

had been able to tell him and from what he had read about Oriental writings, Whitman comprehended that one must learn to love death before he can hope to metamorphose his desire for life (instinct for survival) into a love of life (unconditional approbation of life's totality). To hate death is to hate whatever in life leads to life's decease. But what in life does not contribute to life's cessation? Life is the cause of death. One begins dying from the moment of birth. Man's solid and sullied flesh melts and thaws daily in the quick as well as the dead. Life and death interpenetrate. Life retrieves, in the form of new life, the plunder with which death had absconded; but death, in turn, renews its depredations and the drama is rehearsed *ad infinitum*. Whitman, therefore, will sing death's chants with accents as tender as those with which he sang the chants of life and love. For "what indeed is finally beautiful except death and love?" (*Scented Herbage of my Breast*, p. 84). Whether writing from a profound personal experience or from an aesthetic feeling for the love-death motif, Whitman develops this notion in an unusually poignant fashion. In the second poem in the *Calamus* cluster, we have a thanatopsis recalling *Out of the Cradle Endlessly Rocking* and looking forward to *When Lilacs Last in the Dooryard Bloom'd*. What was to become the "lilac blooming perennial" is here, by turns, the leaves of the sweet flag and the blades of grass growing atop the poet's tomb and, by extension, the leaves which comprise *Leaves of Grass:*

> Leaves from you I glean, I write, to be perused best
>   afterwards,
> Tomb-leaves, body-leaves growing up above me above
>   death,
> Perennial roots, tall leaves, O the winter shall not freeze
>   you delicate leaves,
> Every year shall you bloom again, out from where you
>   retired you shall emerge again.
> O I do not know whether many passing by will discover
>   you or inhale your faint odor, but I believe a few will.
>   SCENTED HERBAGE OF MY BREAST, p. 84

There is no he-bird from Alabama to lament the loss of his mate nor hermit thrush to sing a carol of death. Therefore, the poet will permit the leaves to disclose in their own way what is in his heart. But the leaves no longer convey to him a sense of well-being. On the contrary, they are more bitter than he can bear and they burn and sting him. At the same time, however, they put him in mind of death, which would ordinarily disconcert one engaged in composing chants of lovers. To Whitman, however, death is beautiful. He finds nothing incongruous in offering his love lyrics to death. In fact, he is inclined to believe the high soul of lovers welcomes death most. Does not death guarantee the permanence of plighted troth? Is not death a prelude to the realization of Whitman's ideal of many-in-one, the spiritual utopia whose material counterpart the poet predicted would rise in America? And does not death exempt one from "the weariness, the fever, and the fret" which were as well known to Whitman as to Keats? Suddenly, a new insight is granted the poet: he perceives that love and death are intimately linked, that they constitute the real reality, and that, although presently interspersed throughout life, it may well be that only they will remain when the world of appearances dissolves quite away. Henceforth, therefore, the poet will say the words which can render death exhilirating:

O I think it is not for life I am chanting here my chant of
    lovers, I think it must be for death,
For how calm, how solemn it grows to ascend to the
    atmosphere of lovers,
Death or life I am then indifferent, my soul declines to
    prefer,
(I am not sure but the high soul of lovers welcomes death
    most,)
Indeed O death, I think now these leaves mean precisely
    the same as you mean,
  .   .   .   .
Through me shall the words be said to make death ex-
    hilirating.
Give me your tone therefore O death, that I may accord
    with it,
Give me yourself, for I see that you belong to me now
    above all, and are folded inseparably together, you
    love and death are,
Nor will I allow you to balk me any more with what
    I was calling life,
For now it is convey'd to me that you are the purports
    essential,
That you hide in these shifting forms of life, for reasons,
    and that they are mainly for you,
That you beyond them come forth to remain, the real
    reality.

SCENTED HERBAGE OF MY BREAST, p. 85

This is one of the few instances in which Whitman   84

questioned the actuality of external reality. Even
more important, it is one of the infrequent occasions
when a cry of anguish escapes the essentially
stoical Whitman. Generally, we do not expect the
Bard of Democracy and the hardy, swarthy viator
of the open road to fall upon the thorns of life and
bleed; nor do we expect the great affirmer and
lover to be troubled by the impermanence of
earthly love. Whitman was always completely in
love with "easeful Death," but never, as here, at
the expense of life. Whitman partially recovers his
equilibrium before the *Calamus* cluster of poems is
finished, and, when he again writes of death, it is to
write Lincoln's elegy, where death, as of old, is an
adjunct and not an adjudicator of life. *When Lilacs
Last in the Dooryard Bloom'd* harks back to *Out of
the Cradle Endlessly Rocking*. In the latter poem
(p. 184), death was wooed as "the word final,
superior to all," as "the low and delicious word,"
as "the word of the sweetest song and all songs,"
and as "that strong and delicious word." In the
former poem (p. 237), Thanatos is of feminine
gender and is courted as "lovely and soothing,"
"delicate," "cool-enfolding," "dark mother,"
"strong deliveress," and "loving floating ocean."
And, although Nietzsche abominated the Wagnerian
swoon of death, he joined Whitman in saying that
death was a part of life and not apart from it. In
Joyful Wisdom, he declared: "Let us be on our
guard against saying that death is contrary to life"
(p. 153). And, in *Zarathustra*, he wrote:

85

Everything goes, everything comes back; eternally rolls
the wheel of being. Everything dies, everything blossoms
again; eternally the ring of being remains faithful to itself.
In every Now, being begins; round every Here rolls the
sphere There.

pp. 329-30

For Nietzsche, nevertheless, death could never
assume the importance it did for Whitman who
believed in a life after death. The only future
existence Nietzsche could envision was an identical
reproduction of the earthly existence he had known.
Nietzsche, for example, would not have found any
sense in the following statement by Whitman:

O I see now that life cannot exhibit all to me, as the day
cannot,
I see that I am to wait for what will be exhibited by death.

NIGHT ON THE PRAIRIES, p. 315

Nor would he have subscribed to Whitman's as-
severation that death is "the entrance upon by far
the greatest part of existence, and something that
Life is at least as much for, as it is for itself"
(*Preface*, 1876, p. 434).

The same distinction obtains in their notions of
evolution and eternal perpetuity of human identity.
Eclectic as always, Whitman made his selection
from Emerson, Darwin, and Hegel. The resultant
mélange enabled him to express a belief in a continually motile universe progressively evolving
toward perfection. Though he had his share of
doubts and misgivings regarding the existence of
God and the belief in immortality, not to mention
his inveterate antipathy towards churches, priests,

86

and professional theologians, Whitman maintained to the end that everyone and everything had eternal life. In moments of depression and times of discouragement, he questioned the reality of the physical world and, "half in love with easeful Death," yearned "to cease upon the midnight with no pain." For the most part, however, his earlier works voice his *joie de vivre* and affirm natural passion and the material world, whereas his later works voice his idealism and affirm spiritual values and the immaterial world. The overlap in both directions, of course, was appreciable, and Whitman, to his dying day, insisted on the importance of "physiology from top to toe," and never neglected to render dulia to "Life immense in passion, pulse, and power" (*One's-self I Sing*, p. 5). Whitman came close to Nietzsche when he held that God was incarnated in every human being, but his pantheism also led him to assign purpose to life and to insist that the cosmos is God and God is the cosmos – two notions that Nietzsche never harbored. In some of his hazy formulations of Buddhistic doctrines, such as pre-existence and the unity of past and present, however, Whitman almost anticipated Nietzsche's eternal return.

Whitman knew the tormenting hopelessness of the misunderstood artist and lover as well as the frightful mien of vice and the monstrous visage of evil. But he never suffered the nausea and the fear and trembling that racked Nietzsche. The emotional attrition and the mental anguish which Nietzsche endured in his frantic efforts to find the

87

means of living without God and without the
morality that dies with God were quite foreign to
Whitman. Nietzsche's recusancy drove him to a
nihilistic impasse and to the very edge of the abyss.
Before he could formulate an exultant affirmation,
before he could bridge the abyss, Nietzsche first
had to shape his doctrines of the Superman and the
Eternal Return. Nietzsche's intellectual honesty
compelled him to pursue to the bitter end the
logical consequences of his premises; his yea-saying
is uttered in the very face of life's absurdity,
fortuitism, and naturalism. Whitman, on the other
hand, either through naiveté or through intuitive
wisdom, assumed that life had meaning and meant
good. He devoted his life to proving his assumption. Toward this end, he equably ignored whatever doctrines did not accord with his cherished
convictions, modified some doctrines so that they
did accord, or simply allowed two contradictory
doctrines to stand side by side, confident his ca-
pacious mansion could accomodate one and all.
In Whitman's *En-Masse*, nothing was *de trop*.
Personal tragedy, national tragedy, and ill health
and age inevitably elicited from the poet cries of
grief and sorrow, but Whitman's disenchantments
were always of brief duration and his recovery in
each instance was well-nigh miraculous. The following quotations indicate that Whitman's ideas
regarding the perfection of creation underwent very
little change through the years:

The universe is duly in order, every thing is in its place,

What has arrived is in its place and what waits shall be in
    its place.
THE SLEEPERS, p. 302, 1855

For I do not see one imperfection in the universe,
And I do not see one cause or result lamentable at last in
    the universe.
SONG AT SUNSET, p. 344, 1860

In this broad earth of ours,
Amid the measureless grossness and the slag,
Enclosed and safe within its central heart,
Nestles the seed perfection.
SONG OF THE UNIVERSAL, p. 166, 1874

Life, life an endless march, an endless army, (no halt, but
    it is duly over,)
The world, the race, the soul – in space and time the
    universes,
All bound as is befitting each – all surely going somewhere.
GOING SOMEWHERE, p. 362, 1887

While I cannot understand it or argue it out, I fully
believe in a clue and purpose in Nature, entire and several;
and that invisible spiritual results, just as real and definite
as the visible, eventuate all concrete life and all materialism, through Time.
A BACKWARD GLANCE, p. 453, 1888

Of course, to assess Whitman's thought by reading
his poems in a strictly chronological order is to
disobey the poet's final wishes, and, what is worse,
to incur the danger of misconstruing his final position. Unless one is prepared to argue that Whitman's thirty years' labor in emending and rear-
ranging was undertaken with no regard to the
etiology of his ideas and was prompted by vainglo-
ry, fatuity, senility, or reticence, it might be

prudent to adhere to the order of the ninth (1891-92) edition. Actually, however, no caution is necessary since differences in Whitman's ideas are very frequently more apparent than real, since they are differences resulting from a shift in rhetorical emphasis, from the bias of special pleading, from poetic hyperbole, from a current enthusiasm, or from a transient emotional perturbation. In the above series of quotations, for example, there is only one discrepancy between the chronological order and the order in the ninth edition; and it makes no difference whatsoever. There is nothing which warrants calling Whitman a systematic thinker, but then there are not many literary artists who can lay claim to such a title. Whitman's cosmogony and cosmography may have no scientific validity, yet they are scarcely less plausible than those of other literary cosmonauts such as Milton and Blake.

Whitman believed in an infinite universe continually expanding:

All goes onward and outward, nothing collapses.

I open my scuttle at night and see the far-sprinkled systems,
And all I see multiplied as high as I can cipher edge but the rim of the farther systems.

Wider and wider they spread, expanding, always expanding,
Outward and outward and forever outward.

SONG OF MYSELF, pp. 29; 63, 1855

This universe is composed of matter and spirit: 90

I believe materialism is true and spiritualism is true, I
reject no part.
                    WITH ANTECEDENTS, p. 176, 1860

The total amount of matter and spirit is constant:

Nothing is ever really lost, or can be lost,
No birth, identity, form – no object of the world.
                        CONTINUITIES, p. 361, 1888

Both matter and spirit are eternal:

Nothing ever is or can be lost, nor ever die, nor soul, nor
matter.
                    DEMOCRATIC VISTAS, p. 497, 1871

Time and Space are in endless supply:

See ever so far, there is limitless space outside of that,
Count ever so much, there is limitless time around that.
                        SONG OF MYSELF, p. 63, 1855

These views were held and maintained by Whitman
to the very end. What is more, he never abandoned
his belief in the body and insisted on according it
the same honors accorded the soul. But, tempera-
mentally, especially with the advancing years when
the flames that were wont to "quiver" him to a new
identity were banked and the prods of "libidinous
prongs" had abated, Whitman was too affined to
pantheism, platonism, and transcendentalism not
to lean toward the spiritual. Thus we find him
repeatedly finding a spiritual reality underlying
material appearances:

    Not this the world,
91 Nor these the universes, they the universes,

Purport and end, ever the permanent life of life,
    Eidolons, eidolons.

  .   .   .   .

And thee my soul,
Joys, ceaseless exercises, exaltations,
Thy yearning amply fed at last, prepared to meet,
    Thy mates, eidolons.

Thy body permanent,
The body lurking there within thy body,
The only purport of the form thou art, the real I myself,
    An image, an eidolon.

                              EIDOLONS, p. 9, 1876

A form of Wordsworthian pantheism is evident in
many poems (*Song of Myself*, p. 66, 1855; *On the
Beach at Night Alone*, p. 189, 1856; *Chanting the
Square Deific*, p. 309, 1865; *You Tides with Ceaseless
Swell*, p. 355, 1885; *A Voice from Death*, p. 380,
1891) as is the Emersonian notion that all in time
returns to the divine source from which it came:

Allah is all, all, all – is immanent in every life and object,
May-be at many and many-a-more removes – yet Allah,
    Allah, Allah is there.

  .   .   .   .   .

Would you know the dissatisfaction? the urge and spur of
    every life;
The something never still'd – never entirely gone? the
    invisible need of every seed?

It is the central urge in every atom,
(Often unconscious, often evil, downfallen,)
To return to its divine source and origin, however distant,
Latent the same in subject and in object, without one
    exception.

             A PERSIAN LESSON, p. 381, 1891   92

This "central urge" was, in addition, the property that gave direction to cosmic creation and was apparently capable of recapitulating the entire evolutionary process at will:

There is no stoppage and never can be stoppage,
If I, you, and the worlds, and all beneath or upon their
    surfaces, were this moment reduced back to a pallid
    float, it would not avail in the long run,
We should surely bring up again where we now stand,
And surely go as much farther, and then farther and
    farther.

SONG OF MYSELF, p. 63, 1855

By one of his unique weddings of Darwin and Buddha, Whitman saw each individual as an evolutionary product whose inherited memory contained the experiences of the ancestors from whom he was descended. Insofar as many of man's instincts were unconscious memories of instincts of old, each man could be considered a composite of millions of lives. In each individual, an entire population was summed up and found expression through the expression of the individual. Similarly, inasmuch as each individual transmitted the ancestral and racial memory to future generations, he prefigured future generations' expression of his thoughts by his own expression of them in his time:

I am an acme of things accomplish'd, and I am an encloser
    of things to be.
  .   .   .   .   .

Rise after rise bow the phantoms behind me,
Afar down I see the huge first Nothing, I know I was even
    there,

I waited unseen and always, and slept through the lethar-
gic mist,
And took my time, and took no hurt from the fetid carbon.

Long I was hugg'd close – long and long.

Immense have been the preparations for me,
Faithful and friendly the arms that have help'd me.

Cycles ferried my cradle, rowing and rowing like cheerful
boatmen,
For room to me stars kept aside in their own rings,
They sent influences to look after what was to hold me.

Before I was born out of my mother generations guided me,
My embryo has never been torpid, nothing could over-
lay it.

For it the nebula cohered to an orb,
The long slow strata piled to rest it on,
Vast vegetables gave it sustenance,
Monstrous sauroids transported it in their mouths and
deposited it with care.

All forces have been steadily employ'd to complete and
delight me,
Now on this spot I stand with my robust soul!
SONG OF MYSELF, p. 62, 1855

Not only the evolution of life on the planet earth
but even the evolution of our solar system evidently
cooperated in the conception, gestation, and generation of Walt Whitman, the New Adam, in whom
the Old Adam is dormant and the Future Adam
nascent. To accord with such a magnificently
august notion of nativity one naturally anticipates
an equally superb conception of decease. And
Whitman, of course, is more than equal to the
occasion. As we have seen, he believes in natural

94

immortality, in personal immortality, and in the immortality of identity both as a distinct entity and also as part of the great All. In addition, he believes in some form of reincarnation or return which, at times, sounds very like Nietzsche's eternal return. Both early and late in life Whitman adhered to the orthodox Christian notion of a life after death. His expression reminds us of Tennyson and Dickinson:

My rendezvous is appointed, it is certain,
The Lord will be there and wait till I come on perfect
  terms,
The great Camerado, the lover true for whom I pine will be
  there.

SONG OF MYSELF, p. 63, 1855

Simultaneously he developed the twin notions of the soul's supernatural immortality and the body's natural immortality:

For not life's joys alone I sing, repeating – the joy of
  death!
The beautiful touch of Death, soothing and benumbing a
  few moments, for reasons,
Myself discharging my excrementitious body to be burn'd,
  or render'd to powder, or buried,
My real body doubtless left to me for other spheres,
My voided body nothing more to me, returning to the
  purifications, further offices, eternal uses of the earth.

A SONG OF JOYS, p. 133, 1860

And, ever and anon, he tentatively toyed with either a Pythagorean, Platonic, or Buddhistic theory of reincarnation:

(No doubt I have died myself ten thousand times before.)
SONG OF MYSELF, p. 67, 1855

I feel like one who has done work for the day to retire
awhile,
I receive now again of my many translations, from my
avataras, ascending, while others doubtless await me,
An unknown sphere more real than I dream'd, more direct,
darts awakening rays about me, *So long!*
Remember my words, I may again return,
I love you, I depart from materials,
I am as one disembodied, triumphant, dead.
SO LONG!, p. 350, 1860

Gliding o'er all, through all,
Through Nature, Time, and Space,
As a ship on the waters advancing,
The voyage of the soul — not life alone,
Death, many deaths I'll sing.
GLIDING O'ER ALL, p. 199, 1871

He is closest to Nietzsche when he conceives of the
cycle endlessly recycled as consisting of a beginning,
a purposive progression, a climax comprised of the
attainment of a prefigured end, and a denouement
presaging the recommencement of the drama:

Ever the dim beginning,
Ever the growth, the rounding of the circle,
Ever the summit and the merge at last, (to surely start
again.)
EIDOLONS, p. 8, 1876

There is nothing to indicate that Whitman had a
change of mind as he grew older, but it is true that
one finds less and less mention of a return in his
very last works. Towards the end of his life,
Whitman was more desirous of sailing on and on,

96

forever on, rather than returning. It may be that, like Yeats, he preferred to sail to Byzantium and leave "that country" for good. But in his earlier passion for the "curling grass" he proclaimed with Nietzschean fervor his desire to return and re-experience again and again the madness and joy, the delirious ecstasies of earth, sea, air, and sun:

Ages and ages returning at intervals,
Undestroy'd, wandering immortal,
Lusty, phallic, with the potent original loins, perfectly
   sweet,
I, chanter of Adamic songs.
     AGES AND AGES RETURNING AT INTERVALS, p. 80, 1860

O living always, always dying!
O the burials of me past and present,
O me while I stride ahead, material, visible, imperious as
   ever.
     O LIVING ALWAYS, ALWAYS DYING, p. 314, 1860

By positing an infinitude of time together with conditions conducive to the recurring evolvement of determinate permutations indigenous or affinitive to our ascertained cosmic configurations, it is reasonable to assume that identical beings and events will reappear and repeat indefinitely. Nietzsche made just such an assumption and by so doing arrived at his doctrine of the eternal recurrence. In Nietzsche, no less than in Whitman, the desire for integrity within an eternal context was as compulsive as in any religionist. But, since Nietzsche would not hear of any supernatural constructs or solutions, his task was more formidable than Whitman's. The genius, daring, and agility of

97

Nietzsche's mind, however, was more than equal to
the challenge. By elevating Man-God to the vacat-
ed throne of God-Man, by restoring to the European
pantheon Dionysus and the Eleusinian mysteries
while supervising the removal of Jesus and ersatz
thaumaturges, and by refurbishing in purely naturalistic attire Christianity's best-selling merchan-
dise, immortality, Nietzsche was well on his way to
bridging the abyss Kierkegaard had said could be
negotiated, if at all, only by a death-defying leap.
Eternal recurrence stressed the moment's inesti-
mable value just as the *Übermensch* demonstrated
the individual's infinite worth. God's death had
shattered man's confidence in himself and in life:
without a Divine Will, there can be no Divine Law;
without a Divine Law, there can be no right and
wrong and no supernatural sanctions for moral
precepts; without right and wrong, nothing is true,
all is permitted, and chaos holds absolute sway.
Deprive life of purpose, meaning, and finality, and
it indeed becomes the incoherent bellowing and
manic frenzy of the lunatic. But the eternal recurrence miraculously severs the Gordian knot of
life's absurdity: life's horrors, injustice, transience,
and finiteness are redeemed as soon as man consents
to their eternal return; self-control and order are
instituted anew as soon as man begins to live as he
would wish to live again and again; true freedom,
as understood by Nietzsche, becomes for the first
time possible when man accepts willingly his
inevitable destiny, the only divinity is found to
reside in man's creative faculty for, by saying yes

98

to the world, man becomes not only a yea-sayer and blesser but a creator. In the whole realm of human thought, no idea could have served to express more emphatically the supra-historical outlook and to voice more lyrically the maenadic ecstasy in all that has been, is, and will be, than the idea of the unconditional and infinitely repeated circumrotation of all things. Since, moreover, all things do not recur within the interval of recorded history, Nietzsche even manages to salvage a modicum of purpose and self-determination for man's merely natural and fortuitous empirical self: by overcoming himself, man will serve as a steppingstone to the Superman, and could thus conceivably alter not only his own present destiny but the future of his species as well. Insofar, therefore, as divinizing the earth, the present, and the individual, and insofar as giving assurances of a form of immortality and of the breeding of superior human specimens are concerned, Nietzsche appears to enjoy even more success than Whitman. The eternity he finds in his moment is unobscured by any mystic mists, and the perfection of every moment derives from being's circle which has neither beginning nor end. A *rapprochement* between being and becoming is effected by recognizing that all things are co-present in being and that man's state of being is more important than his purpose or destination. Yet, although Nietzsche's exposition of these ideas discloses a splendid engagement and impassioned rapture, easily vying with Whitman at his most exuberant, his neglect, his solitude, and

99

his ill health hardly permit him to derive any hope from his hope-purveying works. On the contrary, he feels, to employ his own metaphor, like a dispenser of sunlight upon whom no sun shines. He is reminded of the lines of Byron he translated as a youth: "The tree of knowledge is not that of life." To the sister who will later exact a terrible price for her morsel of sympathy, he confesses his solitary existence is a Gethsemane and his knowledge a dead albatross about his neck. Confusing solitude with freedom, except for the temporary relief from excruciating physical pain, the only other happiness he knew was that of the star flung into the "lone chill" and dark stillness of cosmic space.

At the outset, therefore, it is understandable that Zarathustra-Nietzsche fears to admit the idea of recurrence even to himself. He can scarcely contain his revulsion at the mere thought of meaninglessness eternalized. How can one calmly contemplate the perpetual rehearsal of obscene depravities, of diabolic perfidies, of fiendish depredations, of intolerable holocausts? From the reception accorded his previous doctrines, he doubts that man has the courage and strength and honesty to heed one who tells him he must relive eternally the torments he would fain forget. How can one remain undismayed at the realization that one returns "*not* to a new life or a better life or a similar life," but rather "to this identical and self-same life, in the greatest things and the smallest?" (*Zarathustra*, Hollingdale, pp. 237-38).

100

In the second section of *Zarathustra*, in the chapter, "Of Great Events," when his disciples relate that Zarathustra's shadow was seen hurtling through the air and shouting, "It is time! It is high time!" Zarathustra pretends not to understand. In the next chapter, "The Prophet," where his disciples, turned oneirocritics, elucidate one of their master's strange dreams, Zarathustra is again inscrutably silent. And, in the chapter following this, "On Redemption," Zarathustra suddenly breaks off his discourse lest, in speaking of redeeming chance and the past by affirming the present, he reveal all:

> To redeem the past and to transform every 'It was' into an 'I wanted it thus!' – that alone do I call redemption! The will cannot will backwards; and it cannot break time and time's desire – that is the will's most lonely affliction.
>
> .　　　.　　　.　　　.　　　.
>
> The will that is the will to power must will something higher than any reconciliation – but how shall that happen? Who has taught it to will backwards, too?
> But at this point of his discourse, Zarathustra suddenly broke off and looked exactly like a man seized by extremest terror.
>
> ZARATHUSTRA, Hollingdale, pp. 161, 163

But, in this section's last chapter, in a purple patch whose poetic beauty survives even translation, Zarathustra's Athene, the *daimonion* he calls *"my stillest hour,"* materializes in a dream-vision and chides him for behaving like a stiff-necked Moses. And, although she cannot persuade him to embark upon his ministry at once, she leaves confident

101

that, in time, he will recognize his destiny is to be
the teacher of the eternal recurrence:

Something said to me voicelessly: 'You know, Zarathustra,
but you do not speak!'
And I answered at last defiantly: 'Yes I know, but I will
not speak!' ... 'Alas, I want to, but how can I? Release
me from this alone! It is beyond my strength!' ... 'My
words have as yet moved no mountains and what I have
spoken has not reached men.' ... 'They mocked me when
I found and walked my own way; and in truth my feet
trembled then.'

.   .   .   .   .

Then again something said to me voicelessly: 'Of what
consequence is their mockery? You are one who has
unlearned how to obey: now you shall command!'

.   .   .   .   .

And I answered: 'I lack the lion's voice for command.'
Then again something said to me in a whisper: 'It is the
stillest words which bring the storm. Thoughts that come
on doves' feet guide the world.'

.   .   .   .   .

And I considered long and trembled. At last, however, I
said what I had said at first: 'I will not.'

ZARATHUSTRA, Hollingdale, pp. 167-69

Whereupon Zarathustra-Nietzsche, discouraged like
the Whitman of 1860 who was "baffled, balk'd,
bent to the very earth" (*As I Ebb'd with the Ocean
of Life*, p. 185), leaves his friends and once more
retires to his forest fastness.

For this reason, the first full account of the
secret doctrine is reserved for the second chapter of
the book's third section. But, even here, much
remains obscure. Hence, the subject is reviewed in
the concluding chapters of the section. Zarathustra-
Nietzsche, alas, is still subject to violent attacks of

102

nausea. He still cannot bear to think that the loathsome afflictions man and his universe are heir to will continue to occur forever and ever. So, actually, it is Zarathustra's animals who tell him what he has not the fortitude to tell them (Zarathustra, significantly perhaps, is pictured as another St. Francis befriended by the wildlife of the woods, including a lion, an eagle, and a serpent):

'O Zarathustra,' said the animals then, 'all things themselves dance for such as think as we: they come and offer their hand and laugh and flee – and return.
'Everything goes, everything returns; the wheel of existence rolls for ever. Everything dies, everything blossoms anew; the year of existence runs on for ever.
'Everything breaks, everything is joined anew; the same house of existence builds itself for ever. Everything departs, everything meets again; the ring of existence is true to itself for ever.
'Existence begins in every instant; the ball There rolls around every Here. The middle is everywhere. The path of eternity is crooked.'

ZARATHUSTRA, Hollingdale, p. 234

Overcome with emotion, the master expresses his gratitude to his menagerie. He confides that his bitter, oppressive knowledge would have seen the light of day sooner had he been able to reconcile himself to the eternal return of the canaille. But Zarathustra is still convalescing and, although his animals seek to raise his spirits by reciting to him a lecture such as he might deliver on the eternal return, he merely closes his eyes and continues to commune with his soul. Finally, however, Zarathustra-Nietzsche is fully recovered and he celebrates both his rejuvenation and his doctrine in the most dithyrambic verse and saltant prose he ever wrote. Nowhere is the philosopher turned literary artist seen to better advantage than here. It was these chapters that were consulted by Mahler for his Third Symphony and by Delius for his Mass of Life. Serene, confident, and triumphant, Zarathustra-Nietzsche is here at one and the same time the Risen Christ, the reborn Dionysus, Life's Paramour, and the Eternal Walt summoning all of mankind to life's sumptuous feast. He feels at peace with the world and in harmony with all that lives and dies and returns to live again. Now, he is only too eager to impart his wisdom to his friends. He wishes to share the joy and reassurance which the eternal return has afforded him. He wishes to sing, to dance, and to father upon Eternity a child – himself:

If ever my anger broke graves open, moved boundary-stones, and rolled old shattered law-tables into deep chasms:

if ever my mockery blew away mouldered words, and if I came like a broom to the Cross-spiders and as a scouring wind to old sepulchres:

if ever I sat rejoicing where old gods lay buried, world-blessing, world-loving, beside the monuments of old world-slanderers:

for I love even churches and the graves of gods, if only heaven is looking, pure-eyed, through their shattered roofs; I like to sit like grass and red poppies on shattered churches:

Oh how should I not lust for eternity and for the wedding ring of rings – the Ring of Recurrence!

104

> Never yet did I find the woman by whom I wanted children, unless it be this woman, whom I love: for I love you, O Eternity!
> *For I love you, O Eternity!*
> ZARATHUSTRA, Hollingdale, p. 245

Whitman and Nietzsche loved the earth in all its perfect imperfection and in all its imperfect perfection. They affirmed life not only because of their sheer animal faith in life. They hoped their affirmation would encourage a renewal of life and inspire man to progress by the only valid means: by admitting the truths about himself and his destiny. They saw no contradiction between their multilateral love of life and their multiple objection to the vapid, regimentalized existence led by their contemporaries. Man must distinguish between truths intellectually known and truths actually lived; man's scientism cannot afford to dispense with human wisdom. It behooves man to become actually what he is potentially: a human being who recognizes within himself the reflection of the divine wisdom. Man resembles the brute when he accepts life without authentic choices. To their way of thinking, life was disesteemed by the mishmash of otiose laws and taboos mandated by pusillanimous marplots. They called for man's reeducation. Man must be taught to live as he was intended to: devoting his service to "comforts of the sun" rather than to putrescent charnel houses. The divorce of thought and life must cease. Man must accept the earth as all of Gehenna and Xanadu that he will ever know.

105

This is in part what Whitman says when he explains the nature of his lifelong quest:

I was looking a long while for Intentions,
For a clew to the history of the past for myself, and for
    these chants – and now I have found it,
It is not in those paged fables in the libraries, (them I
    neither accept nor reject,)
It is no more in the legends than in all else,
It is in the present – it is this earth to-day.

I WAS LOOKING A LONG WHILE, p. 273

This is no more facile optimism or irresponsible puerility than Pippa's song is a compendium of Browning's philosophy. Whitman knew even better than Pope did that whatever is, should, more often than not, be anything but what it is. He was no more unmindful of the world's materialistic and spiritual evils than William Blake. When Whitman says this is the best of all possible worlds, he does not do so with the impervious conceit and cocksure optimism of a Pangloss or with the harebrained chauvinism of a Grildrig; he does so knowing full well that man conquers his fate by the very simple expedient of loving it at the same time that he admits its inevitability; that man prevails over all the ills he creates for his affliction simply by recognizing they are the counters and forfeits without which life – if life were at all possible without them – would be a flaccid insipidity, a paradise where ripe fruit never falls. That is why Nietzsche, like Whitman, appreciates that his works are not for all readers:

Only the day after tomorrow belongs to me. Some are

106

born posthumously. ... Reverence for oneself; love of
oneself; unconditional freedom before oneself. ...Such men
alone are my readers, my right readers, my predestined
readers: what matter the *rest*?

THE ANTICHRIST, PORTABLE NIETZSCHE, pp. 568-69

Whitman and Nietzsche hated whatever depressed
and debased life. They would have nothing to do
with a twilight or lotus existence. Like Odysseus,
they had to hear the Sirens' song. They had to
immerse in the destructive element. Theirs was the
"heavenly fellowship of men that perish and of
summer morn." Like Thoreau, they felt the need
to front life without civilization's accouterments.
They wanted to know if man could live as one who
loved life without stirring up the blood-lust of
human jackals and cormorants. In their esurience
for experiencing all that human bioplasm can experience, in their insistence on coming to grips with
life free of self-defeating fear and self-deluding hope,
they are like Kazantzakis' Odysseus, who sought
out all forms of life, beyond the limits of rules and
regulations, always mindful of death as a stimulant,
not in order to heighten sensation, but in order to
expend all of himself and to leave to death little, if
any, plunder.

The condition of the patients, man and society,
Whitman and Nietzsche agreed, called for an extensive *débridement*. But, once recovered, the
patients would look back upon their ordeal as well
worth the temporary inconvenience of invalidism.
Theirs would be a higher wisdom than that of
Shelley's Titan; theirs would be the joyous wisdom

107

of men chanting "in orgy on a summer morn / Their boisterous devotion to the sun, / Not as a god, but as a god might be, / Naked among them, like a savage source." In "A Song of Joys," Whitman exposes his eagerness to plunge deep into life's pool and carelessly roil its waters. Like an Achilles aching to launch himself into the middle of the fray, like an impassioned lover burning to quench his ardor's flames, Whitman wants to hurl and spend himself on life's ample breast:

O while I live to be the ruler of life, not a slave,
To meet life as a powerful conqueror,
No fumes, no ennui, no more complaints or scornful
    criticisms,
To these proud of the air, the water and the ground,
    proving my interior soul impregnable,
And nothing exterior shall ever take command of me.

O to struggle against great odds, to meet enemies un-
    daunted!
To be entirely alone with them, to find how much one can
    stand!
To look strife, torture, prison, popular odium, face to face!
To mount the scaffold, to advance to the muzzles of guns
    with perfect nonchalance!
To be indeed a God!

A SONG OF JOYS, p. 133

And, in a remarkably parallel passage, Nietzsche writes:

To be blessed with a strong, bold, and daring soul; to go through life with a quiet eye and a firm step, ever ready for the worst as for a festival, and full of longing for undiscovered worlds and seas, men and Gods; to listen to all joyous music, as if there perhaps brave men, soldiers

108

and seafarers, took a brief repose and enjoyment, and in the profoundest pleasure of the moment were overcome with tears and the whole purple melancholy of happiness: who would not like all this to be *his* possession, his condition! It was the *happiness of Homer*! The condition of him who invented the Gods for the Greeks, – nay, who invented *his* Gods for himself!

JOYOUS WISDOM, p. 236

In omnia paratus, "ever ready for the worst as for a festival," – that is the only way to sally forth to encounter life for the thousandth time. That is the way the Greek, whose attitude toward death Nietzsche admired, sallied forth. The Greeks knew how to die because they never feared to live. Wherever one looks, in their epic poetry, in their drama, in their philosophy, or in their history, one is struck by the positive reverence for life their every posture toward death discloses. Death was never absent from the daily thought and business of the Athenian market-place. It was never omitted from the roll call of festival occasions and national holidays. Significantly, the Greeks had no symbol for death; the cross is of later origin. The Greeks, moreover, never associated death with shame. Generally, death was pictured not as the antithesis of love but as love's handmaid; Pluto, it should be remembered, was an exemplary lover. The notion of visiting deprivations upon themselves to assure themselves of rewards beyond the grave would have struck them as base and foolhardy. The Greeks did not brood over death's other kingdom because they did not inhabit a world of henbane and etherized patients; their last measure of devotion was extended not to cenotaphs but to the human form divine. The only life they were prepared to die for was the life on earth. To return to earth even as a serf, the shade of the haughty Achilles was prepared to give up all. This is the understanding of life and death Zarathustra-Nietzsche wishes to impress upon his friends: they must love the earth more than life itself, but they must also acquire the stoicism to say No when there is no longer time for Yes. They should go to their deaths serenely and triumphantly like Socrates, not cowering in terror before the gibbering palaver of a saffron-robed archimage. They must go to their deaths still blessing life but without any regrets:

Everyone treats death as an important matter: but as yet death is not a festival. As yet, men have not learned to consecrate the fairest festivals.

   .   .   .   .   .

The man consummating his life dies his death triumphantly, surrounded by men filled with hope and making solemn vows.

   .   .   .   .   .

To die thus is the best death; but the second best is: to die in battle and to squander a great soul.
But equally hateful to the fighter as to the victor is your grinning death, which comes creeping up like a thief – and yet comes as master.
I commend to you my sort of death, voluntary death that comes to me because I wish it.

   .   .   .   .   .

That your death may not be a blasphemy against man and the earth, my friends: that is what I beg from the honey of your soul.

110

> Thus I want to die myself, that you friends may love the earth more for my sake; and I want to become earth again, that I may have peace in her who bore me.
>
> ZARATHUSTRA, Hollingdale, pp. 97, 99

Except that Whitman invariably mentioned a life after death, these sentiments will be recognized to be very much the same as his own. Whitman, too, admired the Greeks for "suggesting death in the form of a beautiful and perfect young man, with closed eyes, leaning on an inverted torch – emblem of rest and aspiration after action – of crown and point which all lives and poems should steadily have reference to, namely, the justified and noble termination of our identity, this grade of it, and outlet-preparation to another grade" (footnote in *Preface*, 1876, p. 435). And Whitman, moreover, appears to have died the kind of death Nietzsche proposed to his disciples was the best kind of death: in the midst of his dearest admirers, such as Horace Traubel, Dr. Bucke, and Colonel Ingersoll, Whitman, with Olympian serenity, majesty, and endurance, set sail, on March 26, 1892, toward the promontory where the Great Camerado stood ready to greet and initiate him into the Mystic Order of Adhesiveness. As early as 1871, Whitman had come to view life as the tillage and death as the harvest (*As I Watch'd the Ploughman Ploughing*, p. 316). And in the last year of his life, he respectfully begged to differ with George Inness's gloomy, funereal portrayal of death in the picture, "The Valley of the Shadow of Death." Whitman claims that, from a vast personal experience, he knows

111

that death need not be torturous nor hideous. For his setting, Whitman chooses not the "dank tarn of Auber" and the "ghoul-haunted woodland of Weir," but a Chaucerian meadow filled with the aroma of grass and flowers, sunlight glistening from surfaces recently drenched in sweet April showers:

I make a scene, a song (not fear of thee,
Nor gloom's ravines, nor bleak, nor dark – for I do not
fear thee,
Nor celebrate the struggle, or contortion, or hard-tied
knot,)
Of the broad blessed light and perfect air, with meadows,
rippling tides, and trees and flowers and grass,
And the low hum of living breeze – and in the midst God's
beautiful eternal right hand,
Thee, holiest minister of Heaven – thee, envoy, usherer,
guide at last of all,
Rich, florid, loosener of the stricture-knot call'd life,
Sweet, peaceful, welcome Death.
DEATH'S VALLEY, p. 389

Nietzsche, we have seen, shared every last ounce of Whitman's adoration of effulgent vitality. He, too, believed man's maturity was achieved when he was able to regain the seriousness he had as a child at play. He, too, construed Socrates' 'Know Thyself' and Emerson's 'Trust Thyself' as injunctions to discover oneself by sloughing off the accretions of purblind moralizing and scraping off the encrustations of obsolescent tradition. For him, as for Whitman, the free spirit *par excellence* was the spirit that intuited that there is no increate, and that viewed the inventing of deities as prelusory to the vindication of the only perdurable god –

112

man's self. It was the spirit that delimited its own liberty by creating its own laws and values in order that it might avoid the suicidal anarchy of Karamazov's "all is permitted." It was the spirit that would "sooner murder an infant than nurse unacted desires." It was the spirit that recognized no revelation, no rational axiom bids man do what he ought to do. It was the spirit that, by plunging man into nothingness, sought to create for him the vastness of space, that, by showing him a fathomless world, sought to help him grasp the ground he sprang from. It was the spirit that served the meaning of the earth. It was the spirit that spoke of life as a well of joy and rejoiced in earth's treasures albeit aware of life's pestilences. It was the spirit that said "the earth is like the breasts of a woman: useful as well as pleasing" (*Zarathustra*, p. 319). It was the spirit that bade adieu to life as Odysseus bade adieu to Nausicaa – with a blessing. It was the spirit Zarathustra-Nietzsche sought to instill into his followers when he told them:

Stay loyal to the earth, my brothers, with the power of your virtue! ... Do not let it fly away from the things of earth and beat with its wings against the eternal walls! ... May your spirit and your virtue serve the meaning of the earth, my brothers: and may the value of all things be fixed anew by you. To that end you should be fighters! To that end you should be creators! ... You solitaries of today, you who have seceded from society, you shall one day be a people: from you, who have chosen out yourselves, shall a chosen people spring – and from this chosen people, the Superman. ... Now I bid you lose me and find yourselves; and only when you have all denied me

will I return to you. ... I will be with you a third time,
that I may celebrate the great noontide with you. ... And
this is the great noontide: it is when man stands at the
middle of his course between animal and Superman and
celebrates his journey to the evening as his highest hope:
for it is the journey to a new morning.

ZARATHUSTRA, Hollingdale, pp. 102, 103, 104

Often this spirit is expressed in the works of Whitman and Nietzsche through the metaphors of the
dance and laughter. Dancing, laughing, singing
("I am satisfied – I see, dance, laugh, sing." *Song
of Myself*, p. 27) Whitman and Nietzsche seemed
to be agreed, best captured life's spumescent
ebullience. Whitman and Nietzsche saw them as the
oldest and yet the most eloquent means of denoting
man's cheerful acceptance of life. Song is the systo-
le of life, laughter its diastole, and the dance its
diapason. The dance incorporates what is most
autochthonous in life, as D. H. Lawrence sensed in
watching the snake dance of the Hopi Indians, and
as Nikos Kazantzakis suggests through the inspired
leaps and pirouettes of Macedonian Zorba. The
dance is man's instinctual response to the Dionysian
spirit. It puts to precipitate flight the spirit of
gravity, and renders *hors de combat* the piddling
foes of life with their ratiocinative pother. In *The
Sleepers*, Whitman writes:

I am a dance – play up there! the fit is whirling me fast!
I am the ever-laughing – it is new moon and twilight.
.   .   .   .   .
(It seems to me that every thing in the light and air ought
   to be happy,

114

Whoever is not in his coffin and the dark grave let him
know he has enough.)

pp. 298-99

And Zarathustra, it hardly needs saying, is an
aficionado of the dance and is always picturing
himself as a dancer and a sooth-laugher:

And although there are swamps and thick afflictions on
earth, he who has light feet runs even across mud and
dances as upon swept ice.
Lift up your hearts, my brothers, high, higher! And do
not forget your legs! Lift up your legs, too, you fine
dancers: and better still, stand on your heads!

.   .   .   .   .   .

You Higher Men, the worst about you is: none of you has
learned to dance as a man ought to dance – to dance
beyond yourselves! What does it matter that you are
failures! How much is still possible! So *learn* to laugh
beyond yourselves! Lift up your hearts, you fine dancers,
high! higher! and do not forget to laugh well!
This laughter's crown, this rose-wreath crown: to you, my
brothers, do I throw this crown! I have canonized laughter; you Higher Men, *learn* – to laugh!

ZARATHUSTRA, Hollingdale, pp. 304, 305, 306

If one insists on accepting life without reserve or constraint, one must be prepared to justify every last item in Pandora's box. The iconoclast knows well that iconoclasm invites – if not always the chain, the crag, and the vulture – always revilement, persecution, and a crown of thorns. If one intends to "beat the gong of revolt, and stop with fugitives and them that plot and conspire," (*Song of Myself*, p. 41) he must indeed be possessed of "the faith that never balks" (*Song of Myself*, p. 40). Agonies are one of the rebel's changes of garments and the dramatic fare at the Grand Guignol is the very dough from which the rebel's daily bread is kneaded. "The sworn poet of every dauntless rebel the world over" (*To a Foil'd European Revolutionaire*, p. 262) knows "That he who never peril'd his life, but retains it to old age in riches and ease, has probably achiev'd nothing for himself worth mentioning" (*Song of Prudence*, p. 266). The affirmer of life welcomes every challenge since every challenge enables him to solidify his position by precept and example. Just as the sans-culotte prizes every resistance, token or massive, which augments the tidal wave that will expunge what is rotten at the core and will usher in a spring-like renovation, so life's greatest lovers view every obstacle that stays them from their beloved's bower as fillips to their ardor. It is the traducer of life, the Shaitan for whom earth and earthlings are bitter reminders of long-lost felicities, who is most apt to seize upon life's flaws as major failings and proofs of life's essential labefaction and corruption. The 116 affirmer of life does not emulate the ostrich when danger threatens; he is too honest to resort to evasive action since his very affirmation is largely grounded on his unflinching confrontation of actuality. Instead of refusing to acknowledge life's ills or taking particular pains to emphasize them, he sees them as that strangeness in the proportion which adds materially to the overall beauty. He shows what is deemed detrimental to life is, in the first place, a contradiction in terms (insofar as what is a part of the whole cannot be designated inimical to the whole as long as the whole continues to proliferate) and, in the second place, represents a half-truth which belies the complete truth (insofar as what is deemed detrimental to life, at the same time, nonetheless, stimulates life by generating forces of preservation and renewal).

These were the principal grounds upon which Whitman and Nietzsche found opposition necessary and conducive to life. Whitman arrived at his conclusion largely through his instinctive empathy and sympathy for all. As a measure of his prodigious compassion, he excludes nothing from his all-inclusive, all-approving, benign benediction. Whitman is so confident in the ultimate or basic rightness of almost all things that in the very act of gazing upon earth's suppurating cankers he blesses them unaware. It is not that he regards his nation's ailments as pistareen but that he has learned his lesson complete and knows the wisdom of yielding himself to the perfect whole. Nothing bespeaks Whitman's unquestioning acceptance more than

117

his sublime imperturbability before the shuddering spectacle of swarming evils. While all about him dash helter-skelter recommending radical reforms and proposing extremist measures, Whitman simply remarks all with Jovian insouciance and protracts his yoga-like repose:

I sit and look out upon all the sorrows of the world, and
    upon all oppression and shame,
.   .   .   .
I see the workings of battle, pestilence, tyranny, I see
    martyrs and prisoners,
.   .   .   .
All these – all the meanness and agony without end I
    sitting look out upon,
See, hear, and am silent.
                 I SIT AND LOOK OUT, p. 197

At one time, Whitman ferrets out every fetor and every furuncle both in order to test himself and his resolve and also in order to demonstrate the interchangeability of worst and best:

I do not know what you are for, (I do not know what I am
    for myself, nor what any thing is for,)
But I will search carefully for it even in being foil'd,
In defeat, poverty, misconception, imprisonment – for
    they too are great.
      TO A FOIL'D EUROPEAN REVOLUTIONAIRE, p. 262

And, at all times, as the "extoller of hate and conciliation," (*Song of Myself*, p. 40) he flaunts his non-fastidiousness before the horrified countenances of milquetoasts and celebrates whatever is because it is and because it has always been and will always be. Whitman seldom approximates Frost's con-

118

cision and precision, but he formulated many of Frost's favorite notions before Frost did. Frost's *Evil Tendencies Cancel* summarizes well one of the key ideas in Whitman's philosophy of opposition:

Will the blight end the chesnut?
The farmers rather guess not.
It keeps smoldering at the roots
And sending up new shoots
Till another parasite
Shall come to end the blight.

As has been noted, Whitman often simply denies the existence of the pernicious and pestiferous:

And I will show that there is no imperfection in the present, and can be none in the future,
And I will show that whatever happens to anybody it may be turned to beautiful results.
STARTING FROM PAUMANOK, p. 20, 1860

But this is generally Whitman in the first flush not of callow optimism but of a superabundant, euphoric vitality that found it difficult, if not impossible, to imagine anything irremediably bad. A sadder, wiser, and less vibrant Whitman, acquainted with the murk of internecine civil war, was more philosophical than jubilant though he continued undaunted. What he says of the sea in *With Husky-Haughty Lips, O Sea!* he also applied to himself and his country:

(Naught but the greatest struggles, wrongs, defeats, could make thee greatest – no less could make thee.)
p. 358, 1884

119

His final conclusion (and/or rationalization) was that hardships strengthen resolve, obstacles call forth superior effort, and setbacks whet the appetite for conquest. "Success is counted sweetest / By those who ne'er succeed." Hubristic hunger for experience infinite pulsed through Whitman's arteries with Odyssean imperiousness. And, although the travels of Paumanok's "weary, way-worn wanderer" were, of course, largely mental, they sufficed to teach him that suffering defines happiness, disease engenders the antibodies that insure health, adversity summons noble fortitude, and depression rebels against itself that life may not cease. In *Wandering at Morn,* he compared the Union's successful survival of its intestine ordeal to the thrush which converts the repulsive worms it engorges into melic symphonies of unpremeditated art:

If worms, snakes, loathsome grubs, may to sweet spiritual
    songs be turn'd,
If vermin so transposed, so used and bless'd may be,
Then may I trust in you, your fortunes, days, my country;
Who knows but these may be lessons fit for you?
From these your future songs may rise with joyous trills,
Destin'd to fill the world.

p. 281, 1873

Nietzsche reached similar conclusions through his studies of Greek tragedy which evaluates the protagonist on the basis of the courage and self-integrity he displays in meeting defeat or doom at the hands of the antagonist or fate. Greek tragedy impressed upon Nietzsche that the most crucial

120

question of existence was how to react to adversity and death. By rejecting impassive passivity and accepting a dynamic ethos, Nietzsche had his answer: to love life is to love all life. Originally, he had sought, like so many others, to find a justification for life: and had been forced to the conclusion that life could be justified only as an aesthetic phenomenon. But, by the time he was ready to present *Zarathustra* to the world, his understanding of the matter had altered: he now was positive the proper study of mankind was to love the world rather than to vindicate it. Hereafter, because he regarded every moment as the embodiment of a whole eternity, he taught reverence for the now; and because he regarded Faust's yearning for supernal perfection as unrealistic and nihilistic (very like Edgar A. Poe's quest for the ideal admittedly was), he taught man to perceive that assent to any one thing in life entailed assent to all things. Like Whitman, he believed that, since each being is involved in Being, the rejection of any portion of Being is the rejection of one's own being. One who truly loves life, is not content merely to endure or even to prevail; the true lover insists on an unceasing number of identical repetitions of all that he has ever experienced:

Did you ever say Yes to one joy? O my friends, then you said Yes to *all* woe as well. All things are chained and entwined together, all things are in love;
if ever you wanted one moment twice, if ever you said: 'You please me, happiness, instant, moment!' then you wanted *everything* to return!

you wanted everything anew, everything eternal, everything in love, O that is how you *loved* the world,
you everlasting men, loved it eternally and for all time:
and you say even to woe: 'Go, but return!' *For all joy
wants – eternity!*
ZARATHUSTRA, Hollingdale, pp. 331-32

To love life is to know that even what opposes it
insures its continuance. By imperiling life, life's
adversaries inspire a posture of defense, security
measures, and retaliation which assure life's future.
Diseases are exigent in their exactions and defeats
rankle terribly. Once weathered, however, they are
the best guarantee that all will yet be well and that
the forts of folly may indeed soon fall. Furthermore, since Nietzsche was inclined to see life as a
circle rather than a straight line of infinite length,
he came to see eye to eye with Whitman: nothing
found in life can be said to be permanently fatal to
life since life has been exposed to identical conditions an innumerable number of times without
suffering serious impairment or curtailment. The
ascetic, Spartan, and stoic traits that led Whitman
to practise frugality, self-denial, and self-discipline,
led Nietzsche to extract from a life-long ordeal of
sickness, neglect, and loneliness, a philosophy of
life much closer to that of Robert Browning than to
that of Arthur Schopenhauer. In his theory of the
superior man, he made clear he expected the Overman to overcome his theroid instincts, to subjugate
his unruly desires, to sublimate the impulses of the
id, and to direct his will-to-power to the enlighten-
ment rather than enslavement of man. In other

122

words, the principal clue to the nature of Nietzsche's Overman was self-conquest. Just as the fiercer the forge flame, the finer the temper of the Toledo blade, so, Nietzsche believed, the harsher the afflictions and privations overcome, the more hardy, sturdy, ennobled, and magnificent the character of those who overcame them:

> The highest type of free men should be sought where the highest resistance is constantly overcome: five steps from tyranny, close to the threshold of the danger of servitude. ...Danger alone acquaints us with our own resources, our virtues, our armor and weapons, our *spirit*, and *forces* us to be strong – otherwise one will never become strong.
> TWILIGHT OF THE IDOLS, PORTABLE NIETZSCHE, p. 542

Whitman and Nietzsche were at great pains to make known to their would-be disciples that the regimen they would impose would be rigorous to the point of hardship. Only those who welcomed rebuffs, who were renewed by defeats, who knew fear but conquered fear, who saw the abyss yet remained undismayed – only such could hope to pass the entrance examinations set for admission to the open air academies of Whitman and Nietzsche. Whitman tells those who would follow him they must be prepared to give up all and must stand ready to withstand all manner of privation. Unless they are willing to save themselves by exposing themselves to all that is mortal and unsure, it were better that they stayed at home to reap the plenteous harvest which is the hire of self-denying conformity:

> The way is suspicious, the result uncertain, perhaps destructive,

123

You would have to give up all else, I alone would expect
    to be your sole and exclusive standard,
Your novitiate would even then be long and exhausting,
The whole past theory of your life and all conformity to
    the lives around you would have to be abandon'd.
    WHOEVER YOU ARE HOLDING ME NOW IN HAND, p. 86

He going with me must go well arm'd,
He going with me goes often with spare diet, poverty,
    angry enemies, desertions.
              SONG OF THE OPEN ROAD, p. 115

Nietzsche sternly states that he will have nothing
to do with sunshine rebels or with shilly-shallying
casuists. In existentialist vein, Nietzsche asks his
students to drink deep or taste not the Sisyphean
Spring. Since every triumph presupposes an obstacle, a hurdle that has to be hurdled, Nietzsche
wishes for his pupils an obstacle course dotted with
traps and ambuscades. He wishes for them the
encounter with the most dread of all foes – nihilism.
He wishes for them the travail of those who intuit
for the first time that life has no meaning other than
the meaning freely imposed by them themselves.
He wishes for them the self-mortification that shall
lead not to a pessimistic and passive acquiescence
in the purposelessness of existence but to the emer-
gence of a higher type of man:

Type of my disciples. To those human beings in whom I
have a stake I wish suffering, being forsaken, sickness,
maltreatment, humiliation – I wish that that profound
self-contempt, the torture of mistrust of oneself, and the
misery of him who is overcome, not remain unknown to
them: I have no pity for them because I wish them the

124

only thing which can prove today whether one has worth or not – that one holds out.

NOTES, 1887, PORTABLE NIETZSCHE, p. 456

Just as necessity is the mother of all invention, and obstruction the proving ground of all hardiness, so, Whitman believed, success is the prelude to new exertions; success is the synthesis, so to speak, soon to become thesis and soon to be challenged in turn:

Now understand me well – it is provided in the essence of things that from any fruition of success, no matter what, shall come forth something to make a greater struggle necessary.

SONG OF THE OPEN ROAD, p. 115

It is of this self-same "greater struggle," which safeguards and nourishes the vital instinct, that Nietzsche is thinking when he writes:

Ask yourselves whether a tree which is to grow proudly heavenward can dispense with bad weather and tempests: whether disfavor and opposition from without, whether every kind of hatred, jealousy, stubbornness, distrust, severity, greed, and violence do not belong to the favoring circumstances without which a great growth even in virtue is hardly possible?

JOYFUL WISDOM, p. 56

Whitman and Nietzsche agreed that man's ability to cope with whatever posed a threat to his individuality had to be cultivated continually. Both would have said that man could do much worse than emulate Faulkner's Old Ben, "an old bear, fierce and ruthless, not merely just to stay alive, but with the fierce pride of liberty and freedom,

125

proud enough of that liberty and freedom to see it
threatened without fear or even alarm; nay, who at
times even seemed deliberately to put that freedom
and liberty in jeopardy in order to savor them, to
remind his old strong bones and flesh to keep
supple and quick to defend and preserve them."
Whitman shouts at the top of his lungs that he
instigates warlike rebellion, that he incites men to
riotous resistance, that he harbors hunted outcasts,
that he urges daring defiance of accepted norms,
that he mistrusts luxury and overrefinement:

My call is the call of battle, I nourish active rebellion.
SONG OF THE OPEN ROAD, p. 115

I am he who tauntingly compels men, women, nations,
Crying, Leap from your seats and contend for your lives!
.   .   .   .
Fear grace, elegance, civilization, delicatesse,
Beware what precedes the decay of the ruggedness of
    states and men.
BY BLUE ONTARIO'S SHORE, p. 242

To these sentiments, Nietzsche subscribed wholeheartedly:

Illness may even act as a powerful stimulus to life, to an
abundance of life. It is thus that I now regard my long
period of illness: it seemed then as if I had discovered life
afresh, my own self included. I tasted all good and even
trifling things in a way in which others could not very
well taste them – out of my Will to Health and to Life I
made my philosophy. ... For I wish this to be understood;
it was during those years of most lowered vitality that I
ceased from being a pessimist: the instinct of self-recovery
forbade a philosophy of poverty and desperation.
ECCE HOMO, MODERN LIBRARY, p. 820

126

Nietzsche agreed with Whitman that what does not kill man makes him stronger. He, too, believed all strong natures require resistance to attain full fruition and to fulfill themselves completely. "Everything decisive arises as the result of opposition." (*Ecce Homo, Modern Library*, p. 894). Suffering is frequently one of the principal roads to perfection. Nietzsche and Whitman knew the secret of Homer's Greeks, knew how to rejoice in the midst of tragedy. To retain his grip on reality man requires external stimuli. Sensory deprivation or overstimulation leads to personality disintegration which may eventuate in madness or death. To stress the need for equable orientation almost to the exclusion of the need for sensory excitation, as Whitman and Nietzsche felt religious and societal conventions did, was to gamble rashly with the health of the human organism.

As one might expect, Whitman and Nietzsche found physical illness a stimulant rather than a depressant to their cosmic eulogizing. Viewed from atop the Magic Mountain, life irradiates a preternaturally luminiscent lambency. Plot alone does not suffice to explain why the warm, youthful passion of Porphyro and Madeline is consummated against the backdrops of cold, death, and old age. The interest in, and insistence on a sensuous apperception of external reality (common to Keats, Whitman, Nietzsche, D. H. Lawrence, and Hemingway, among others) connotes a passionate love of life, a yearning to conquer the Conqueror Worm. Whitman confides to us that the paralysis and anorexia of his senescent days enables him to appreciate all the more the joyful paeans he endited when he was in better health:

> I occupy myself, arranging these pages for publication, ... under the physical affliction of a tedious attack of paralysis, obstinately lingering and keeping its hold upon me, and quite suspending all bodily activity and comfort. I see now, much clearer than ever – how much my former poems, the bulk of them, are indeed the expression of health and strength, the sanest, joyfullest life.
>
> Footnote in PREFACE OF 1876, p. 435

And Nietzsche, in a characteristically brilliant insight, says the suffering his precarious health periodically subjected him to is responsible for the tenor of his philosophy:

> As my inmost nature teaches me, whatever is necessary – as seen from the heights and in the sense of a *great* economy – is also the useful par excellence: one should not only bear it, one should *love* it. *Amor fati:* that is my inmost nature. And as for my long sickness, do I not owe it indescribably more than I owe my health? I owe it a *higher* health – one which is made stronger by whatever does not kill it. *I also owe my philosophy to it.*
>
> NIETZSCHE CONTRA WAGNER, PORTABLE NIETZSCHE, p. 680

According to the Gospel by Dostoievski, happiness can be attained only through suffering; according to the Gospel by Whitman and Nietzsche, suffering is a form of happiness. If, on the Emersonian lintel the motto was 'Whim,' on the Whitman-Nietzsche lintel, the motto read: 'What destroys me not, strengthens me.'

To both writers, eudaemonism was a bête noire.   128

Cold Pastorals are in the repertoire of neither Whitman nor Nietzsche. Their songs sing of boughs that bid the Spring adieu with cheerful optimism rather than bleak despair, of brimming beakers of sangaree that set at naught both mistral and sirocco. To Whitman and Nietzsche, unheard melodies are sweet, but heard melodies are sweeter still. And the sweetest of all are the ones sung fortissimo, the ones danced to Terpsichore's wildest measures. In the place of the fusty fulminations of pandits and pundits, Whitman and Nietzsche recommend reality's caves of ice and sunless seas. In their total assent to total life, they find the ululations of woman wailing for her demon lover as sweet as the tunes of Attic pipes and timbrels, as lovely as the strains plucked from dulcimers by Abyssinian maids. Life, whatever its golgothas, must not be despised; the challenge of Polyphemous must be answered. The great noon, eternal spring are blackest midnight's and Boreas' first-born. It is out of such knowledge that the Future, which shall belong to the undaunted Camerado and the intrepid Overman, will be born. Failure defines success; disappointed ambition furnishes the formula for conquest; rank injustice extirpates the pernicious craving for justice; torture teaches the scorn of pain; woes infinite yield to joys ineffable:

Whatever we do not attain, we at any rate attain the experiences of the fight, the hardening of the strong campaign, and throb with currents of attempt at least. Time is ample. Let the victors come after us. ... There is an immortal courage and prophecy in every sane soul that cannot, must not, under any circumstances, capitulate. *Vive*, the attack – the perennial assault! *Vive*, the unpopular cause – the spirit that audaciously aims – the never-abandon'd efforts, pursued the same amid opposing proofs and precedents.

DEMOCRATIC VISTAS, p. 472

Nietzsche stresses the fact that noble souls disdain the easy conquest. He points out that the successes of your enemy become your successes when you have the honesty to admit you were wrong. He explains that, although earthquakes visit havoc upon humanity, they at the same time elicit humanity's best, the subtle brotherhood of men often established by an open boat ordeal. He offers the reassurance that despair itself is often the initial stage to a position of strength where one refuses to delude himself with lies:

If something great has failed you, does it follow that you yourselves are failures? And if you yourselves are failures, does it follow that *man* is a failure? ... The higher its type, the more rarely a thing succeeds. ... Have you not all failed? Be of good cheer. ... How much is still possible!

Midnight too is noon; pain too is a joy; curses too are a blessing; night too is a sun.

ZARATHUSTRA, pp. 404; 435

It was in this light that Walt Whitman, as we have suggested, came to view and justify (at least to himself) the Civil War. Among his stirring reveilles, impressionistic verse vignettes of battles and soldiers, and recitatives detailing his experiences in the hospitals among the wounded, the poet finds time to see the War of the States as a proving 130 ground; as the momentary descent to Avernus indispensable to the attainment of the Newest Atlantis; as the arduous contest from which the *agonistes* emerges crowned with laurel:

> Long, too long America,
> Traveling roads all even and peaceful you learn'd from
> joys and prosperity only,
> But now, ah now, to learn from crises of anguish, advanc-
> ing, grappling with direst fate and recoiling not.
> LONG, TOO LONG AMERICA, pp. 222-23

Whitman, clearly, was not one of those parlor soldiers whom Emerson berated for shunning the rugged battle of fate. The above lines, from *Drum-Taps*, 1865, practically paraphrase Emerson's entry in his *Journal* for November, 1862:

> Well, this is the task before us, to accept the benefit of the War; it has not created our false relations, they have created it. It simply demonstrates the rottenness it found. We watch its course as we did the cholera, which goes where predisposition already existed, took only the susceptible, set its seal on every putrid spot, and on none other; followed the limestone, and left the granite. So the War.

Much of what Whitman and Nietzsche had to say regarding good and evil has been anticipated in considering their attitudes towards contradiction and opposition. Aggressive vitalists that they were, they naturally inclined strongly to the view that good consisted of life's allies and evil of life's enemies. At the same time, as we have observed, they were prepared to defend, and anxious to proclaim their belief that life's enemies were as necessary as life's allies for life's continuance. In addition, their personalism once more led them to Emerson's door. The latter's sentiments in *Self-Reliance* clearly anticipate the conviction held in common by Whitman and Nietzsche that, what is inimical to self, is evil, and that, what is partial to self, is good:

No law can be sacred to me but that of my nature. Good and bad are but names very readily transferable to that or this; the only right is what is after my constitution; the only wrong what is against it.

Finally, it was to be expected that, since they were life's apologists, they should accept, and even love all aspects and conditions of life, including what was customarily designated evil. Contradiction, of course, would not have disturbed them. But, actually, they saw no contradiction in embracing evil even if it were defined as inimical to their selves, for it will be recalled that, what opposed the self, was deemed salutary to the self by both writers. Both construed morality almost exclusively in terms of vitality. Their distance from Hemingway

132

in this regard is more apparent than real. Life itself
absorbed their attention more than life's earnest-
ness or life's meaning. Life's spectacle engrossed
them. But they wanted to be actors in that spectacle just as much as they wanted to contemplate and
analyze its drama. All their thinking predicated
that man and existence are desirable, worthwhile,
and wonderful; and that the strife of direct opposites is a condition of life. Believing in life's forked
flame, they believed that nothing was retrogressive
that helped guard against the flame's extinction.
They shared Blake's convictions that everything
that lives is sacred, that Contraries are necessary
to human existence, and that energy is eternal
delight. Nietzsche put it as follows:

If I have proof that error and illusion can serve the development of life, I shall say 'yes' to error and illusion; if it
has been demonstrated to me that the instincts styled
evil by the morality of the present, – for example, hardness,
cruelty, ruse, daring audacity, combative temperament
are likely to increase man's vitality, I shall say 'yes' to
evil and sin.

THE ANTICHRIST, PORTABLE NIETZSCHE, p. 637

The experiencing of an ecstatic joy from an apperception conditioned by a spectator relationship to
existence is a matter of temperament – just as its
opposite, say in the case of Schopenhauer's pessimism, is. Given such a temperament – a philosophy
of life which views the vital instinct as the most
precious of all things – one can anticipate much of
what will be adduced to vindicate such a tempera-
133   ment's faith. No arguments perhaps have been as

frequently rehearsed as those called forth by one whose commitment to the vital instinct is total. For the latter type of individual, personalism is as much the *organon* as ratiocination was for the *Aufklärung* and its subsequent reincarnations. Rationalism and anti-rationalism are at one in their humanism and humanitarianism: they share alike the belief in man's essential goodness and in human nature's infinite perfectibility. They also agree that, this being the case, man's abortive endeavors at self-expression and the confluence of factors denying the fulfillment of his birthrights are wholly society's fault, and hence contingent and remediable. Both of these attitudes towards life, moreover, are not only strongly optimistic concerning man's fate, but also disclose, by this very optimism, their tender solicitude for man and their incurable idealism. Both attitudes desire the instantaneous rearing of paradise on earth and both are confident the feat may be accomplished purely through human agency. They are realists in recognizing sweeping changes must be made and much of the old must be discarded; yet they are blithedalers in thinking the improving of society will improve man.

Where they differ is in the means they believe best calculated to effect most quickly their longed-for improvements. Obviously, the regnant idols of the partisans of logic are science and induction, whereas the ruling penates of the devotees of instinct are art and intuition. One's sanctum sanctorum is knowledge; the other's is the life force. The rationalists follow Socrates in saying the rational principle should enjoy the governance of the passionate principle. The anti-rationalists protest against this arbitrary suzerainty which they contend is nocuous to the integral personality; they accuse the rationalists of foolhardiness in trying to shape man into what he cannot be and into what he was never intended to be. The rationalists are partial to the Apollonian: their religious thought, regardless of how much or how little of miracle and revelation it admits, is generally arrived at through logic – whether it be Moses' Torah, Socrates' theism, Aquinas' Roman Catholicism, Leibnitz's deism, or Kant's natural religion. The anti-rationalists favor the Dionysian – whether it be the wisdom of the Prophets, the sacrarium of Isis, the mysticism of Swedenborg, the pantheism of Rousseau, the Christianity of Berdyaev and Kierkegaard, or the existentialism of Camus.

Their most strenuous efforts by far are exerted in justifying man and man's life. Toward this end, both schools of thought address themselves with all the ingenuity at their command. For, although, deep down in their unconscious, there is perhaps the inadmissible knowledge that one cannot justify the unjustifiable, neither school dares confess what would indeed prove life to be the meaningless tale of an idiot. Neither doubts that life will cease the moment it cannot be justified. Consequently, both agree that the problem of evil has to be disposed of if all proofs in defense of life are not to be invalidated.

135   As everyone knows, however, any concerted at-

tack against evil or any undue concern with it arouses suspicion. People wonder whether one may not be protesting too much. Freudian self-consciousness has permeated all to such a degree that diffidence by itself can no longer be taken as the sole cause of the grave misgivings aroused by any ardent plea. The sceptic cannot refrain from inquiring why the affirmers of life's splendors so often speak in accents which, although not those of despair, are, more often than not, couched in terms of euphoric megalomania. Is not the obsession to demonstrate that life is not absurd a measure of the fear with which purposeless existence is contemplated? Did Camus succeed in persuading himself in *The Myth of Sisyphus*? Is not the Bosom Serpent gnawing inside all who pen testaments of life, all who, like Billy Budd, react more paroxysmally in affirming cosmic justice precisely because they were initially nonplused by the world's evil – is not this hateful reptile fear?

Such obstinate questionings do not have to be the *nugae* of a *flâneur* or the disaffirmances of a nihilist. What is more, they can be ignored only at the risk of distortion. Fortunately, however, as we shall see, Whitman and Nietzsche themselves dispose of most of them. And those not disposed of thus can be dismissed by pointing out that, when disillusionment is made accountable for Swift's satire and fear of death explains Hemingway's novels, nothing is really explained except the limitations of the would-be explicator. The charge of relativism, moreover, is false when one levels it against

136

a man who says that a context can be contrived for anything to prove it is whatever one wishes it to be. Whitman and Nietzsche make this very point. In addition, where Whitman and Nietzsche are concerned, there is merit not only in the fact of utterance but also in the felicity and cogency of the utterance. Last, it should be recognized that one cannot affirm life without first judging it; and that it is impossible, most of the time, to judge without being led to condemn. Nevertheless, as Whitman and Nietzsche teach us, since man is able to write both of the affirmation and the condemnation, he can master life. And, as long as man can do that, he has done all: he has given purpose to life – to the same extent that the work of an artist has purpose, to the same extent that the artist imposes purpose upon his creation.

This is the awareness at the core of Whitman's and Nietzsche's notions of good and evil. Both were personalists. What they approved of was called good. What promoted the welfare of the vital instinct was called good. What tended to teach and encourage individualism was called good. Good was love of man through love of self. Good was the worship of man's creations. Good was everything that loved life. Good was birth, growth, and death. By the same tokens, evil was whatever they disapproved of. Evil was whatever was hypocritical, contumelious, sinistrous, circumspect, abjectly conformist, over-solicitous of tradition, fearful of innovation, predisposed to inertia, meanly pragmatic, egregiously authoritarian. Self-doubt, self-denial, and self-betrayal were cardinal sins in the eyes of both Whitman and Nietzsche.

Total assent and acceptance of all life was Whitman's credo. Indifference to life, one possible definition of nihilism, was, where Whitman was concerned, the worst form of treason and blasphemy. Likewise, passivity was as hateful to Whitman as to Blake. His all-enveloping sympathy included in the sunshine of its affection lamb and tiger, innocence and experience, woman and man, good and evil. He found positive values in existence and positive values in society. Therefore, he had no hesitation in setting down life's curses alongside life's blessings; he recorded society's shameful doings as well as society's noble doings. Whitman was closer to Hawthorne than to Emerson in perceiving how dangerous it was to deny human imperfection; he did not foolishly demand a monistic ethos in the face of cosmic pluralism. Although his diction inclines towards absolutes and extremes, Whitman subscribed to the principle of reasonable culpability. Paumanok's child was always the rebel rallying free souls under the banner of nonconformity. He stood neither above men nor apart from them. The faith which found "perfect and clean the genitals previously jetting" (*The Sleepers*, p. 302) refused to be balked by any room or dweller in life's mansion:

(Shall I make my list of things in the house and skip the house that supports them?)

I am not the poet of goodness only, I do not decline to be the poet of wickedness also.

138

What blurt is this about virtue and about vice?
Evil propels me and reform of evil propels me, I stand
    indifferent,
My gait is no fault-finder's or rejector's gait,
I moisten the roots of all that has grown.
  .   .   .   .
I find one side a balance and the antipodal side a balance.
SONG OF MYSELF, p. 40

Like the Christ who compassionated Magdalene and
the adulteress, Whitman plead the case of the
insulted and injured. He believed empathy was the
only morality. Hence every pariah and derelict
was dear to him. He blessed them all in full
awareness. Were they any the less individuals for
being outcasts? Had they yielded up integrity of
self any more than had the eminent men who had
suborned and groveled in order to rise to a great
place? Every man's humiliation, every man's de-
gradation, every man's imprisonment, every man's
self-apostasy, diminished Whitman. He, too, was
one well acquainted with the night. Therefore, he
sought not to know for whom the tocsin clanged;
he knew it clanged for him:

Lusts and wickedness are acceptable to me,
I walk with delinquents with passionate love,
I feel I am one of them – I belong to those convicts and
    prostitutes myself,
And henceforth I will not deny them – for how can I deny
    myself?
YOU FELONS ON TRIAL IN COURTS, p. 272

He felt the staid, safe virtues of the mollycoddled
and sanctimonious had to be superseded by the
impulses of the self if life's springs were not to run

139

dry. From the rejected he demanded the strength born of rejection. Man's power, he taught, derives from the knowledge of his fallibility. To his followers, he recommended the less traveled roads, the most difficult paths, because it is only by overcoming opposition that man becomes aware of his full potential:

> Negative qualities, even deficiencies, would be a relief. Provision for a little healthy rudeness, savage virtue, justification of what one has in one's self, whatever it is, is demanded.
>
> DEMOCRATIC VISTAS, p. 478

By this logic, Whitman was able to approve even what is generally designated as forbidden. For, although he believed in heaven, he emphatically rejected the notions of hell and purgatory. All, he was certain, would ultimately be redeemed. Consequently, he was not alarmed by the fact that good and evil appeared inseparable. He refused to tolerate any twaddle about reprobation and original sin. He looked upon religion's tools for salvation as supererogatory albeit adiaphorous. He believed the only true redemption was self-redemption, which was achieved not by obeying abstract moral commandments but by giving ear to one's own *individuum*. Man is lost the moment he begins to look for rules and regulations to direct his thoughts and actions. For morality's codes all too often aim at reducing the freedom of choice to the minimum, which is usually no choice at all. Whitman believed in moral responsibility which seeks to extend rather than to

140

delimit the individual's range of free choices. To
Whitman, human wickedness was to be ascribed
to sickness, mental aberration, or society's materialism and unnatural restrictions rather than to
innate depravity. Man's value was ascertained not
by his goals or even by his achievement; it was
determined by his effort, by how he weathered
defeat and frustration, by how much he loved man.
At Whitman's festive board are invited all and
sundry because all and sundry are involved in
mankind and because all and sundry have thought
evil if they have not actually perpetrated evil:

> With music strong I come, with my cornets and my
>   drums,
> I play not marches for accepted victors only, I play
>   marches for conquer'd and slain persons.
> .   .   .   .   .
> This is the meal equally set, this the meat for natural
>   hunger,
> It is for the wicked just the same as the righteous, I make
>   appointments with all,
> I will not have a single person slighted or left away,
> The kept-woman, sponger, thief, are hereby invited,
> The heavy-lipp'd slave is invited, the venerealee is invited;
> There shall be no difference between them and the rest.
>   SONG OF MYSELF, p. 37

All too frequently those who deny the freedom of
the will evince an instinctive aversion to the evil
deed and the evildoer to the same degree that their
opponents, the believers in free will, do. But
Whitman, accused by many of a lack of intellectual
sophistication, was above such sophistry. He understood Christ better than many erudite theologi-

141

ans when he envisioned the Great Camerado for-
giving all, without a single exception, on Judgment
Day. In the superb future whose coruscating
brilliance he seemed to glimpse as a distant star,
Whitman foresaw the harmonious blend and merge
of all into a wonderful, perfect unity. In the
meantime, however, he was more than ready to
accept life's antimonies in all their irreducible
polarity. Although he believed in a hereafter and
was convinced that life displayed abundant signs
of meaning, purpose, and progression, he still clung
to the idea that the enlightened individual possessed total freedom and total responsibility. Although his affirmation of life was as resounding as
the last movement of Beethoven's Fifth Symphony,
he seldom lost sight of the evil and suffering all
about him. And, although he was positive Blake's
Jerusalem would be rebuilt upon earth, he did not
hesitate to urge his followers to follow Tannhäuser's
example – to reject paradise and return to the
world of men:

The difference between sin and goodness is no delusion,
The earth is not an echo, man and his life and all the
    things of his life are well-consider'd.

You are not thrown to the winds, you gather certainly and
    safely around yourself,
Yourself! yourself! yourself, for ever and ever!
.   .   .   .   .

How beautiful and perfect are the animals!
How perfect the earth, and the minutest thing upon it!
What is called good is perfect, and what is called bad is
    just as perfect.

TO THINK OF TIME, pp. 306; 308   142

Complete and exalted allegiance to the earth must
become man's faith since it already is his fate.
Only he who has seen through man's illusions and
simultaneously has recognized man's need for illusion is truly enlightened, free, realistic, and responsible. Everyone, whether he wills it or not, is
a collaborator in cosmic destiny. It behooves man
to immerse himself in the destructive element, to
see life's evil steadily and to see it whole. To refuse
to do so is to repudiate the testimony of the senses.
To refuse to do so is to deny the real life and say yes
to an imaginary one. To refuse to do so is to fail to
see that reality lies not beyond appearances but
within them. Even though answers may not be
ready at hand, man must not curb his questing
spirit, must never cease seeking and striving.
Though there may be abundant reasons to doubt it,
life has meaning and means good:

I know now why the earth is gross, tantalizing, wicked, it
    is for my sake,
I take you specially to be mine, you terrible, rude forms.

(Mother, bend down, bend close to me your face,
I know not what these plots and wars and deferments
    are for,
I know not fruition's success, but I know that through
    war and crime your work goes on, and must yet go on.)
                BY BLUE ONTARIO'S SHORE, p. 251

One may be influenced to say yes to life either
because he believes or does not believe in a creation
by design and/or with design. Nietzsche, paradoxically, had to affirm all because he repudiated
all: that is to say, although his affirmation was not

143

based upon nihilism, nihilism was its starting point. Nietzsche's love of life is predicated upon, and is fomented by cosmic fortuitousness. Nietzsche angrily poured an avalanche of scorn on the notion that man's life was given him as a gift to serve a purpose lying outside of himself. The only order and meaning Nietzsche could discover in the universe was the order and meaning men attributed to it or imposed upon it. He did not believe that life acquired meaning because it served an impersonal external purpose. Nietzsche found life's meaning in the fact of life itself. Whitman's love of life, on the other hand, – and here we have a major point of difference – proceeded from his belief in an educated and sane purpose behind creation:

While I cannot understand it or argue it out, I fully believe in a clue and purpose in Nature, entire and several; and that invisible spiritual results, just as real and definite as the visible, eventuate all concrete life and all materialism, through Time.

A BACKWARD GLANCE O'ER TRAVEL'D ROADS, p. 453

One can never say yes to life, however, if he does not have confidence in man's willingness and ability to recognize himself as the master and creator of his own good and evil. Faith in man makes it possible for one to say yes to evil and no to evils since it both presupposes and defers the radical melioration of human nature. One cannot help but note that the unforced cheerfulness of Whitman and Nietzsche stems from the certainty, to which both tenaciously adhere, that man can will and will will to follow their directions for a halcyon

144

future. Clearly, although one can live without hope for himself, one can scarcely live without hope for the race. Nietzsche's affirmation hinges on man's being able to summon the resolve necessary to pursue constructive goals in the face of cosmic nullity; man's potency lies in his ability to confront his impotency. Whitman's affirmation rests on the trust he places in man's inveterate determination to countervail the ills his humanity subjects him to:

> Judging from the main portions of the history of the world, so far, justice is always in jeopardy, peace walks amid hourly pitfalls, and of slavery, misery, meanness, the craft of tyrants and the credulity of the populace, in some of the protean forms, no voice can at any time say: "They are not." The clouds break a little, and the sun shines out – but soon and certain the lowering darkness falls again, as if to last forever. Yet is there an immortal courage and prophecy in every sane soul that cannot, must not, under any circumstances, capitulate? *Vive*, the attack – the perennial assault! *Vive*, the unpopular cause – the spirit that audaciously aims – the never-abandon'd efforts, pursued the same amid opposing proofs and precedents.
>
> DEMOCRATIC VISTAS, p. 472

Hope is endemic to the majority of humankind. Even more than life itself, man desires reasons for living. That is why Whitman and Nietzsche feel at ease in their adoration of what exists; they know such adoration cannot be deemed preposterous so long as it does not abrogate their right to call for certain reforms and changes. One justifies not only his own existence but life itself when one refuses to be either the accomplice or the silent witness of

145

evil. By the same token, one can do no greater harm to life than to order one's existence according to some lost paradise or future heaven. All too often, when man surrenders to illusion, magic, and the miraculous, he ceases to struggle. All too often, when man loses his way in a fictitious fog of ideals, he is unable to think clearly, and he is apt to forget that he himself created those ideals to serve his own ends. All too often, when man permits society to fit him with spectacles which show things to be arbitrarily all white or all black, his perception of reality is dulled and he may scarcely discern evil though it stare him in the face. Culturally inherited orientations screen man from reality and thus deprive him of the most tried and proved weapon against evil – truth.

Whitman would have found little to quarrel with in Nietzsche's conviction that man can know good and combat evil only if his words, thoughts, acts, and wishes are his own, only if his volition remains unencumbered by anything extrinsic to itself. Like Nietzsche, Whitman's notions of good and evil were shaped, consciously and unconsciously, by Christ's teachings. But, of course, both writers interpreted Christ's message in their own manner. Occasionally, Whitman would rant against vice and sinners in the manner of an Old Testament prophet. For the most part, however, he was no more uneasy about evil than he was about God and immortality. Instead of fretting over it, arguing about it, seeking to define it, attempting to separate it from the good, Whitman was of the opinion that

146

man should triumph over it by living fearlessly and confidently. The man who owns only himself master gladly embraces what is inevitable, gladly consents to all that is problematic and strange in the double wisdom that whatever is is necessary and exists only by life's permissiveness. To love the inevitable and the unalterable is the highest wisdom and freedom within man's finite power. When man concedes the ineluctable evil and injustice that are in him, in others, and in the world, he defines a dialect of confrontation. Then and only then is he ready to commence a new quest for clarity, truth, justice, and bortherhood. Whitman would undoubtedly have endorsed Hawthorne's observation in *The Marble Faun:* "While there is a single guilty person in the universe, each innocent one must feel his innocence tortured by that guilt."

Whitman was aware twenty centuries had not lessened the sum total of evil in the world. He knew that pure virtue was no more compatible with life as he knew or could conceive it than unalloyed cynicism was. He knew that man was neither completely innocent nor entirely depraved. He knew that even after man reformed himself and society within the realm of possible reform, utopia would still be a dream. At the same time, however, Whitman knew that to abstain from warfare against evils because of nihilistic despair constituted arrant infidelity to the human condition. He knew that the individual achieves perfection not by self-denial and by imitation of tradition but by self-expression and self-realization. He knew the worst evil was to ignore evil, to minimize its threat, or to endure it passively. He knew that when one forgets the present for the future, he no longer loves life. The key issue in Goethe's epic drama is not whether Faust will or will not be saved. The real question is whether Mephistopheles will or will not induce Faust to deny the significance of life and the purposefulness of Faust's own being. Whitman knew that the flesh is weak, that the majority of men are like Faust: that they can love Gretchen and Helen – humanity and art – for a spell but are unable to live without the 'lies' of the socially conditioned perception they have become addicted to. That is why he was insistent that man must learn to penetrate beneath and through society's deceptions. He knew that the real provision for the future consisted in giving all to the present. But one must never forget that Whitman's present was a present discovered by the Whitmanian vision rather than by the astucious astigmatism of society:

I have heard what the talkers were talking, the talk of the
    beginning and the end,
But I do not talk of the beginning or the end.
There was never any more inception than there is now,
Nor any more youth or age than there is now,

And will never be any more perfection than there is now,
Nor any more heaven or hell than there is now.
.   .   .   .   .

Showing the best and dividing it from the worst age
    vexes age,
Knowing the perfect fitness and equanimity of things,
    while they discuss I am silent, and go bathe and
    admire myself.

SONG OF MYSELF, p. 26   **148**

The moment contained all the promise and reward that mortal and compassionate man could legitimately wish and covet. The means and the end of life, as well as the reciprocal justification of the one by the other, were all carried within the pregnant womb of the present. The plenum of proof for inscrutable destiny's sentience, and the banner under which mankind might be well advised to learn to live and to die resides paradoxically in non-human creation:

I think I could turn and live with animals, they're so
        placid and self-contain'd,
I stand and look at them long and long.

They do not sweat and whine about their condition,
They do not lie awake in the dark and weep for their sins,
They do not make me sick discussing their duty to God,
Not one is dissatisfied, not one is demented with the mania
        of owning things,
Not one kneels to another, nor to his kind that lived
        thousands of years ago,
Not one is respectable or unhappy over the whole earth.

SONG OF MYSELF, p. 47

Whitman can feel for the discouraged, the defeated, and the disappointed because he, too, has known adversity, because he, too, has been smitten hip and thigh by that serpentine albino cetacean, because he, too, has experienced the Gehenna of desolation and utter loneliness. He, too, searched for meaning in meaninglessness; he, too, sought for pause amid vortiginous mutability; he, too, hungered for love's certainty on a darkling plain. Every man carries within him his own desert places.

149

But duty to self as well as to neighbor demands that he fight these arid wastes in himself as well as in his fellow man. The mere wish for immortality testifies to life's meaning and to life's meaning good. Man must never cease fighting against that in himself of which he is afraid. The Future is what the Past will change into, and the Present is the changing – which is the human race's being, the moment of truth. Man's ever-renewed and ever-defeated effort is not in vain; it is his happiness and triumph if he will but recognize it as such:

Be at peace bloody flukes of doubters and sullen mopers,
I take my place among you as much as among any,
The past is the push of you, me, all, precisely the same,
And what is yet untried and afterward is for you, me, all
    precisely the same,
I do not know what is untried and afterward,
But I know it will in its turn prove sufficient, and cannot
    fail.

SONG OF MYSELF, p. 61

Nietzsche scorned all forms of transcendence, whether moral or divine, because, to his way of thinking, transcendence leads to slander of this world and this life. Nietzsche argued that only the discontented took refuge in an imaginary, fictitious other world; only the vulturine priests, prompted by neuroticism or cupidity, sought to weaken and stunt man's delight in living by telling him that to obtain the true life he must deny the real life. Whitman, however, regarded transcendence as the greatest testimonial of life's value. Transcendence was Whitman's means of making this mortal and

150

limited world preferable to any other. It was his
means of saying yes and no to life simultaneously:
yes to its growth and no to its tabescence. The
only *esclandre* for Whitman was the renunciation
of human complicity. He never approved of mere
lip service to life's demands; he felt they had to be
lived and acted upon. For Whitman the praise-
worthy individual was he who asserted his identity
without lapsing into egocentricity, whose thoughts
and acts issued from out of his own being, whose
life's task was to cultivate his creative self. Whitman would have agreed with Hawthorne that the
only unpardonable sin was the sin of Ethan Brand;
his individualism was neither a narcissitic pre-
occupation with his own ego nor the hoity-toity
refusal on the part of an exhibitionist to be one of
hoi polloi. Nietzsche gagged at the mere thought
of pity and D. H. Lawrence was disgusted with
Whitman's preachments on sympathy. Be that as
it may, Whitman's ideas on the magnetic chain of
humanity are not essentially different from those
found in such diverse works as *The Rime of the
Ancient Mariner, Moby Dick, The Marble Faun,
Crime and Punishment,* and *Victory.*

For Whitman, life's horrors were not death and
despair but doubt and tyranny. He did not feel
that to love life and man was to approve centuries
of injustice and murders. To consent to what must
be was to be sensible, realistic, and courageous. To
pledge allegiance to the eternal present was to discard illusory hopes and hopeless illusions. Despite
his idealism and mystical pantheism, of which he

151

availed himself or not as the whim of a particular day dictated, Whitman was practical enough to realize that what never had real existence in this life and never could was scarcely calculated to prove a boon to mankind. Though he might oppugn death's dominion with the orotund accents of Dylan Thomas and serenade life's orange and green with the verbal magic of Wallace Stevens, it became more and more apparent to Whitman that the greatest labor of his life was to reconcile man to the ash heaps and stony images that outraged one's eyes wherever he turned. Daily he witnessed tradition's failure to light the way; daily he heard "the Chimney sweeper's cry," "the hapless Soldier's sigh," and "the youthful Harlot's curse." Daily he beheld the comic yet tragic spectacle of the professors at the Academy of Lagado energetically plying their trade and completely unmindful of the fact that reason can offer man no reason to live. Whitman's humane sentiments together with his passion for truth and his trying personal experiences would not permit him to dismiss the problem of evil lightly. Those who contend he lacked the vision of evil have read him superficially or not at all. The existence of evil troubled Whitman almost as much as the fact of death. But his affirmative outlook soon persuaded him that there was really nothing to fret about. Evil was part of the ensemble that Whitman loved so passionately. Hence, like death, it was to be celebrated rather than deprecated. Moreover, in time, the evolutionary process would dispose of it altogether:

152

For it the mystic evolution,
Not the right only justified, what we call evil also justified.
.   .   .   .   .

Out of the bulk, the morbid and the shallow,
Out of the bad majority, the varied countless frauds of
    men and states,
Electric, antiseptic yet, cleaving, suffusing all,
Only the good is universal.
.   .   .   .   .

From imperfection's murkiest cloud,
Darts always forth one ray of perfect light.
SONG OF THE UNIVERSAL, pp. 166-67

We thus see that it is not out of indifference or insensitivity that Whitman is able to catalogue the ills of life with Buddhistic impassiveness. Rather it is because he believes that ultimately evil shall have no dominion. After reading Hegel, he came to understand evil as being part of the antithesis which would engender the utopian synthesis:

Roaming in thought over the Universe, I saw the little
    that is Good steadily hastening towards immortality,
And the vast all that is call'd Evil I saw hastening to
    merge itself and become lost and dead.
ROAMING IN THOUGHT, p. 198

Nietzsche does not have substanially more to add. His doctrine of beyond good and evil is not a license for licentiousness and libertinism. He is not advocating Ivan Karamazov's 'Everything is permitted.' Nietzsche was not so naive or depraved that he failed to appreciate the necessity for new values and laws to replace those which God's death had invalidated. Although he did wage a vigorous crusade against traditional permissives and prohibitions, against placebos of the hereafter variety, and against all creators and values not directly of human issue, anarchy was no more Nietzsche's aim than it was Whitman's. Both were always mindful of the dangers and pitfalls that could easily attend the rule of conscienceless individuals and men-Gods. Both displayed a diathesis for the superman, but never for a moment lost sight of the fact that one of its manifestations is the subhuman. Whitman anticipated Nietzsche in warning that, without Law and Conscience, none of his reforms could be implemented and brought to fruition. Whitman did say that the prime task of Democracy was to vindicate Individualism and the Individual, but he does not say that the best government is no government:

The purpose of democracy – supplanting old belief in the necessary absoluteness of establish'd dynastic rulership, temporal, ecclesiastical, and scholastic, as furnishing the only security against chaos, crime, and ignorance – is through many transmigrations and amid endless ridicules, arguments, and ostensible failures, to illustrate, at all hazards, this doctrine or theory that man, properly train'd in sanest, highest freedom, may and must become a law, and series of laws, unto himself, surrounding and providing for, not only his own personal control, but all his relations to other individuals, and the States; and that, while other theories, as in the past histories of nations, have proved wise enough, and indispensable perhaps for their conditions, *this*, as matters now stand in our civilized world, is the only scheme worth working from, as warranting results like those of Nature's laws, reliable, when once establish'd to carry on themselves.

Democracy too is a law, and of the strictest, amplest kind. 154

Many suppose (and often in its own ranks the error), that it means a throwing aside of law, of running riot. But, briefly, it is the superior law, not alone that of physical force, the body, which, adding to, it supersedes with that of the spirit. Law is the unshakable order of the universe forever; and the law over all, and law of laws, is the law of successions; that of the superior law, in time, gradually supplanting and overwhelming the inferior one.

DEMOCRATIC VISTAS, pp. 464-65; 469

Nietzsche distrusted the state more than Whitman did, but he would not have found very much to quarrel with in the above passage. Nietzsche designated good whatever was creative instead of traditional, whatever danced with wild abandonment to the intangible and ineffable tarantella of life, whatever accepted proudly the burden of incertitude and inevitability, whatever was self-seeking and self-assertive rather than self-demeaning and self-denying. His keen appraisal of human nature proved to him that what the Superman – (who, it cannot be repeated too often, was closer to Emerson's 'individualist' than Carlyle's 'hero') – willed was good. Nietzsche believed that he who possessed vitality and genius and who was unhampered by a deity's commandments, by categorical imperatives, or by a superego (shaped by social customs and herd prescriptions) not only exemplified goodness but also virtually defined what was good by whatever he did or did not do. Nietzsche called good not the man without conscience but the man whose conscience was instinctual and fashioned by his own observations. Bad conscience was explained by Nietzsche as the curse visited

155

upon all originality voiced in a society enslaved by the despotic heel of tradition. Evil is whatever depresses life's volant volatility, whatever debases life's splendent sublimity. Evil is the hatred of the this-worldly, the traducing of the passion for utter truth and honesty. Evil is whatever is insentient, illusory, or nihilistic. Moreover, since the conditions which engender, incubate, harbor, and promote being vary and can never be thought of as absolutes, good and evil are at best expedient labels of nomenclature useful when, at any specified confluence in time and space, conditions both beneficial and detrimental to life may be differentiated. It is self-evident that "good and evil that are not transitory, do not exist" (*Zarathustra, Portable Nietzsche*, p. 228). The free man (who, in Nietzsche, it must be resaid, is the enlightened man, not the criminal) recognizes the herd's arbitrary hair-splitting as spurious. He rejects it with the same instinctive aversion he rejects the illusion on which it is erected – the promised justice and reward outside of time. For, by virtue of their ineluctable relativeness, good and evil obviate their legitimacy as value criteria within the eternal flux:

All things have been baptized in the well of eternity and are beyond good and evil; and good and evil themselves are but intervening shadows and damp depressions and drifting clouds.

ZARATHUSTRA, PORTABLE NIETZSCHE, pp. 277-78

As previously observed in another connection, Nietzsche always opposed what appeared to him as the false distinction between this world, identi-

156

fied with merely phenomenal reality, and the world
beyond, identified with transcendent reality which
was presumably truly eternal and really real.
Nietzsche argued that it was all too easy to lose
sight of the sacredness and innate nobility of life
if one sustained himself solely on the hope that the
world beyond would compensate him for the losses
and failures he endured in this world. In his up-
goings and downgoings, Zarathustra, like Gulliver,
learned that the title of Nardac, the highest honor
Lilliput could bestow, was an empty honor in
Brobdingnag or in England. One man's meat may
be another man's poison; lilies that fester smell far
worse than weeds. Nietzsche contended that the
truly enlightened individual warred against the
notion of ideals just as he warred against sickness.
The Superman, totally liberated in himself, does
not continue locked in time and history; he does
not inhibit and imprison himself by the belief that
he will reach perfection only if he directs himself to
higher goals. Nietzsche believed man must arrive
at a sense of identity independent of social struc-
ture and in contradiction to it. For man to discover
his true self, which was inaccessible to socially
conditioned perception, man must, like Zarathustra,
first alienate himself from society and thus see
through society's self-deception and orientative illusions. The myth of eternal verities is just that –
a myth! There is only verity – and verity, whether
one chooses to call it vice or virtue, good or evil, is
purely the product of temporal, geographical, ethnic, and racial conditions:

157

> Much that was good to one people was scorn and infamy
> to another: thus I found it. Much I found called evil here,
> and decked out with purple honors there.
>
> ZARATHUSTRA, PORTABLE NIETZSCHE, p. 170

This was the logic on which Nietzsche based his prediction that, one day, good would cease to be done for moral reasons.

As Whitman did before him, Nietzsche saw much which was unspeakably ugly and loathsome in the world, but this did not diminish his love of life one iota more than it did Whitman's. As in Whitman's case, his love and faith were strengthened rather than undermined by the spectacle of the *lex talionis*. For him, as for Whitman, evolution was not an illustration of a death struggle for survival, but a triumphal pageant of life's irreparable serendipity and irrepressible proliferation:

> In nature the state of distress does not *prevail*, but super-
> fluity, even prodigality to the extent of folly. The struggle
> for existence is only an *exception*, a temporary restriction
> of the will to live; the struggle, be it great or small, turns
> everywhere on predominance, on increase and expansion,
> on power, in conformity to the will to power, which is just
> the will to live.
>
> JOYFUL WISDOM, p. 290

D. H. Lawrence's worship of the sun (and the life quickened by its briefly illuminating but unbearably brilliant rays) was shared alike by Whitman and Nietzsche. Both would have agreed with Wallace Stevens that "After the final no there comes a yes / And on that yes the future world depends. / No was the night. Yes is this present

158

sun" (*The Well Dressed Man with a Beard*). Whitman and Nietzsche perceived, as Lawrence did after them, that it was man's fear of death that made him recoil with horror from the more violent and passionate proofs of vitality. Although they did not falsify life by equating it too readily with intensity of physical sensation, for them, the seething cauldron of life was great beyond all gods. Zarathustra feels that the evocation of the grotesque and sinister affirms life as much as the celebration of life's gemmy splendors. To Zarathustra, primeval chaos, dumb, unassuageable grief, a cicatricose world thrashing about with the torment of some inscrutable fatality, also conveyed an overwhelming sense of life:

I am delighted to see the wonders hatched by a hot sun: tigers and palms and rattlesnakes. Among men too a hot sun hatches a beautiful breed. And there are many wonderful things in those who are evil.

There is much filth in the world; that much is true. But that does not make the world itself a filthy monster.
ZARATHUSTRA, PORTABLE NIETZSCHE, pp. 255; 317

Which is not to say Whitman and Nietzsche embraced evil as their good, or indulged in the romantic paralogism of glorifying crime and childishly defying some unconscious (or, in the parlance of the pathetic fallacy, malignant) Almighty Ogre. The one important respect in which neither can be identified with the Romantic Rebel, the Great Defier, or located in the camp of the Satanists, is that, instead of bitterly resenting man's lot, each is more than well pleased with it. Each desires to

159

have the play reperformed endlessly; each shouts *bravissimo* and not only to the play but also to the players. Whitman and Nietzsche sought no Faustian pacts and found little to admire in the hero-villains of Vigny and Lermontov. They deemed themselves above worship of the chimerical and regarded Comstockery and the blasphemy of what exists as the despicable avocation of the *flâneur* or the petty petulence and malice of the impotent and demented. Their answer to the unhappiness in the world was not to augment it; their answer to the evil in the world, to the millions caught and exposed in Eichmann glass cages, to the millions foundering in Kafkian nightmares, to the millions suffering the agonies of Tennessee Williams' characters, was good deeds. Whitman (to the great annoyance of D. H. Lawrence) opined that "whoever walks a furlong without sympathy walks to his own funeral drest in his shroud" (*Song of Myself*, p. 66); and Nietzsche, though he theoretically scoffed at humanitarianism for the same reasons he deplored traditional Christianity, proved, with his last lucid act of embracing a noble Houyhnhnm (a gesture Swift would surely have appreciated) that he actually was all compact of the milk of human kindness. Like the Matthew Arnold of *Dover Beach*, Whitman and Nietzsche were not unduly alarmed at the prospect of Christianity's death because they knew that the salient truth Christianity symbolized, the triumphant suffering of man, would live on and help mould man into one whom fate could never surprise nor death ever dismay.

160

Of course, any power ethic that exalts vitality with Spartan ruthlessness invites an inhuman, or, at the least, a non-human rationale which is irrational in the very exorbitancy of its rationalism. Nietzsche's perfervid infatuation with lucidity eventuated not only in his own alienation but to a collective European insanity that has left the world, as it did Freud, baffled to the point of suicidal despair. Nevertheless, it is difficult not to agree with Albert Camus that, to the credit of his philosophical integrity, Nietzsche faced up to the logical consequences of his reasoning without flinching. In contrast to Whitman who, in one passage, calls to his banner only the healthiest of the healthy, and, (faithfully adhering to his love of contradiction) in the following passage, summons to his colors all and sundry, including the degenerate and the debilitated, Nietzsche has no qualms in consigning to extermination those who would jeopardize the evolution of overman. Mindful that George B. Shaw was equally adamant where the Life Force was concerned, and bearing in mind that in Nietzsche's psychological construct pity always loomed as the greatest temptation (*Zarathustra, Portable Nietzsche*, p. 439), one may understand, even if one cannot agree with Nietzsche when he writes:

What is good? Everything that heightens feeling of power in man, the will to power, power itself.
What is bad? Everything that is born of weakness.
What is happiness? The feeling that power is *growing*, that resistance is overcome.
Not contentedness but more power; not peace but war;

not virtue but fitness (Renaissance virtue, *virtù*, virtue
that is moraline-free).
The weak and the failures shall perish: first principle of
our *love* of man. And they shall even be given every
possible assistance.

THE ANTICHRIST, PORTABLE NIETZSCHE, p. 570

By 'war' Nietzsche, of course, means intellectual
not physical conflict. Nor should it be forgotten
that he, too, loved contradiction. In one place, for
example, he was able to say (and thereby play into
the hands of the Rosenbergs of the world): "When
the ends are great, humanity employs other standards and no longer judges crime as such even if it
resorts to the most frightful means." (Quoted by
Albert Camus in *The Rebel*, Alfred A. Knopf, New
York, 1956, p. 77). Yet, almost in the same para-
graph, he could confess: "It is easy to talk about
all sorts of immoral acts; but would one have the
courage to carry them through? For example, I
could not bear to break my word or to kill; I should
languish, and eventually, I should die as a result
– that would be my fate" (*Ibid.*, p. 77).

In general, the animus behind most of Nietzsche's
reflections on good and evil is the ethic of personalism rather than the ethic of the power elite.
From first to last, Nietzsche never stops reiterating
that man must overcome himself: must, that is,
liberate himself from the trammels and the shackles
of the herd; must achieve the conquest of fear,
which demeans life, and the conquest of humility,
which insults life. Every prospective candidate for
matriculation in the service of Zarathustra is sub-

162

jected to the scrutiny of the same question: "Can you give yourself your own evil and your own good and hang your own will over yourself as a law?" (*Zarathustra, Portable Nietzsche*, p. 175). Man's duty is to challenge and reassess everything anew; his highest calling is to be an energumen of life. So long as man fails to shoulder the onus of his own good and evil, mankind is left without a goal. So long as man abstains from grasping the reins of creation; so long as he does not comprehend that they are even now in his hands, waiting on his will, he remains a slave. So long as he chooses the cloudy palm of Olympus instead of the April green of Ithaca, he continues the dupe of superstition, the ally of illusion, and the traitor of life:

What is good and evil *no one knows yet*, unless it be he who creates. He, however, creates man's goal and gives the earth its meaning and its future. That anything at all is good and evil – that is his creation.

ZARATHUSTRA, PORTABLE NIETZSCHE, p. 308

Until man breaks the old tablets, he is mired in the past, fails to adjudicate the present, and abdicates from his responsibility to the future. One becomes the creator of good and evil only by first destroying all values. Falsehoods regarding man's biological nature, and rationalizations for man's infirmities must be seen clearly for what they are. Truth in all her ragged harshness must be pursued and wooed assiduously and without constraint. All moral values based on misty idealism and not grounded on concrete reality must be scourged from life's temple. The virtue which proceeds from ignoring

163

or denying nature is no virtue at all; it is the worst of vices. The only evil is that which conceals and distorts truth, that which by imposing an imaginary meaning on life, prevents the discovery of its real meaning:

> Everything that the good call evil must come together so that one truth may be born. O my brothers, are you evil enough for this truth? The audacious daring, the long mistrust, the cruel No, the disgust, the cutting into the living – how rarely does all this come together. But from such seed is truth begotten.
>
> ZARATHUSTRA, PORTABLE NIETZSCHE, p. 312

The consideration which directs Zarathustra to teach that "Man must become better and more evil," (*Zarathustra, Portable Nietzsche*, p. 400) is the same consideration which influences Odysseus to identify himself and to taunt the tormented Polyphemous – thereby jeopardizing an escape well-nigh accomplished.

The peculiar intensity of emphasis many pretend to discover in the staunch advocacy of male friends in Whitman and Nietzsche can be shown – where it is not an undigested gob of pruriency in the pretenders – to be entirely logical and quite normal. After all, an Ancient Mariner will always reserve a special room in his heart's mansion for that wedding guest who gratifyingly listens without benefit of mesmeric coercion. Christ at Gethsemane has consoled many poets and philosophers, among others, who failed of a receptive hearing in their own day. The touching devotion of his pupils and friends contributes immensely to the ritualistic solemnity of Socrates' trial and death, which contain all the terrible beauty of a classical Greek tragedy.

Few passages in Whitman and Nietzsche are more moving than those which disclose their oppressive sense of loneliness. Like the mental flights of Blake, the mecca to Walden Pond by Thoreau, the voyages to the South Seas by Melville, the erethistic peregrinations of D. H. Lawrence, Whitman's and Nietzsche's imaginary journeys – which they are continually tramping, always, like the prophets of old, carrying a staff – emphasize their need for a friendly hearing as well as their state of solitariness. Whitman's raucous appetency for gregariousness bespeaks his gnawing sense of aloneness. Nietzsche's Zarathustra invariably interrupts his enforced santon-like existence to return to the city and once more sharply attack the mindless somnolence of doltish man. Each found and failed to find in mental motion the reassurance and tranquillity

165

which Hawthorne, another one-time resident at
Solitude Hostelry, found through Sophia Peabody.
Whitman's threnody on Lincoln (wherein the melancholy of bereavement is attenuated by the lyric
articulation of *amor fati*) voices a preternatural
sense of sundering as do Nietzsche's reflections on
his break with Wagner. In both instances, the fact
that the emotion is authentic yet disproportionately
magnified, calls attention to the unsatisfied desire
for companionship, and helps explain the extreme
lengths (surrogate objects, fictive creations, ethnic
and universal identifications) each vainly employed
to fulfill his exigency for an understanding friend.

Anxious for an audience, and convinced, with the
cocksureness of genius, of their right to an audience,
nay, of the world's danger should it fail to grant
them an audience, it is understandable that Whitman and Nietzsche should, when refused the ears
of the many, seek, if only in reverie, for the select
few who might appreciate them. Like Christ,
Whitman and Nietzsche construed brotherhood
literally as man's love for man. More than likely, it
was asceticism rather than inversion that led them
to believe the love of man for man, unmotivated
(or so it seemed to them) by vanity, convention, or
connubial and concupiscent notions, could be more
noble and altruistic than love of man for woman.
Furthermore, all precedents directed that disciples
be of male gender; history and male chauvinism
enjoined that the shapers and men-gods of the
future, though woman-born, be men. It is naive to
attribute to Whitman and Nietzsche a prejudice

166

of Western Civilization which antedates Christianity by several centuries. In addition, it may be
pointed out (although Mrs. Anne Gilchrist and the
female devotees and votaries of D. H. Lawrence
might be cited in the way of refutation) that the
athletic programs and outdoors regimens of Whitman and Nietzsche (aside from being vague and
visionary rather than pragmatic and practicable)
were scarcely geared to my lady's tastes and talents.
The conditions and environs under which Whitman
and Nietzsche would have felt most at ease and
would have been able to breathe most freely, would
not have seemed particularly felicific to most cats,
women, and wives. Though he may give himself
over entirely to the effort, one is sure to experience
difficulty in attempting to visualize a maenadic
German Countess swirling through a czardas with
Zarathustra. Nor is it easier to picture an Emily
Dickinson, without reserve or constraint, strolling
with eurythmy on Broadway, Whitman's left hand
hooking her round the waist, his right hand pointing to landscapes, while she chants an antiphonic
accompaniment to his mostly spry, occasionally
torpid measures. Shaw's New Woman not yet
having been evolved Whitman and Nietzsche pru-
dently, albeit with many a backward glance, sought
out Siegfrieds only, in the certain knowledge that,
wherever Siegfried went, Brünnehilde would be sure
to follow.

Scabrous succubi, *soi-disant* literary analysts,
have, like insolent Catilines, abused our patience
long enough. When they tell us Whitman's cele-

167

bration of the friend is anything more or anything less than a protest against the cruelty, hypocrisy, deceit, and callousness inhering in the relations between man and his fellow, they speak less than truth. Such cozeners were rebuked (although, alas, not for once and for all) by Whitman himself:

The special meaning of the "Calamus" cluster of *Leaves of Grass* ... mainly resides in its Political significance. In my opinion, it is by a fervent, accepted development of Comradeship, the beautiful and sane affection of man for man, latent in all the young fellows, North and South, East and West – it is by this, I say, and by what goes directly and indirectly along with it, that the United States of the future ... are to be most effectually welded together, intercalated, anneal'd into a Living Union.
Footnote in PREFACE, 1876, p. 438

Whitman's verse bears out this prose pronouncement in every particular. Love, respect, and reverence of the friend was to Whitman and Nietzsche love, respect, and reverence of the self and the self in the friend. To Whitman, as to Nietzsche, love was more than the procreative urge; to both, it was the kelson of creation, the leaven from which would spring the breed of sun-delighting gods the whence of whose past and the whither of whose future would be testified to only by the dew upon their feet:

I will sing the song of companionship,
   .   .   .   .

I will write the evangel-poem of comrades and of love,
For who but I should understand love with all its sorrows
    and joy?
And who but I should be the poet of comrades?
STARTING FROM PAUMANOK, p. 17

168

Ultimately, we return to the myth of Prometheus. For was it not love of man that inspired the first rebel's rebellion? And was it not this same love that innured humanity's staunch champion to undeserved torture, that strengthened the energy of his resolve to continue his defiance of Zeus, that ennobled his agonies, that taught man the most "godlike crime was to be kind"? Among people of great intelligence and sensitivity, the inclination towards vagabondage, fostered by a distaste for a society dependent for its existence on orientative illusions, continually conflicts with the inclination towards gregariousness, fostered by the deeply tragic insight into man's fallibilities and man's dubious gift to be able to be at once the subject and object of his meditations. Like Pascal, Swift, and Stevenson, among others, Whitman and Nietzsche saw quite lucidly man's degeneracy as well as man's nobility. Though they assailed many of man's vices, his supererogatory twaddle of categorical imperatives, and his topsy-turvy constructs of just and unjust, their faith in man's essential worthiness and in his ability to become better remained as firm as the Rock of Gibraltar. They loved man for himself, not only because they were human themselves. At the same time, they recognized that man's fate would increasingly depend on his maintaining harmonious, considerate, compassionate relations with other men. For, despite all his symbols, and tokens, and organizations, and relationships, suggesting companionability, sociability, and brotherhood, they perceived man was dreadfully,

169

desperately "alone, alone, all, all alone." That is one reason why the notions of love and friendship figure so conspicuously in their work.

The cartoons of his day did Whitman scant justice in depicting him as a roly-poly Falstaff or as one of the Cheeryble brothers. More introspective than extroverted, more tender than robust, more compassionate than erotic, more pathetic than insolent, more profound than naive, more delicate than agrestic, more sensitive than lusty, he was more the man of sorrows than he was Pantagruel. A savior in search of salvation, a messiah in search of a people, Whitman devoted so many of his omnivorous lines to love because the fear of loneliness is often more terrifying than the fear of death. Throughout his work, he consistently and most appropriately uses the metaphor of Cupid's life-affirming handiwork to give expression to his Personalism, to make clear his belief that, until man learns to see his fellow man as a distinct identity, different from, but not subordinate to his own identity, he gropes in a Minoan maze, the wandering outlaw of his own dark mind. Whitman held that love unified all existence. Participation in the act of love he viewed as the symbol of a deeper participation, of participation in cosmic unity and human unison. The man-hating, life-despising, no-saying Minotaur, Nihilism, daily devours him who has not attained self-trust and self-mastery, who has not acquired the courage to love his fellow man. In Whitman's eyes, Blake's Satanic Mills and Lawrence's accursed machines were not

170

irreparably, if at all, Satanic and accursed. Whitman's religion did not exclude the industrial phase of life. He believed industrialism could be both beneficial and beautiful. (Whitman anticipates Hart Crane, Carl Sandburg, T. S. Eliot, and Stephen Spender, among others, in finding the industrial scene a fit subject for poetry.) But he insisted that human relations be exempt from commercial considerations; that man's relation to man always take precedence over man's relation to the machine. If he were remembered for anything, Whitman wished to be remembered for his all-embracing love. For is not the measure of the intensity of love, measure, also, of earth's verve?

Recorders ages hence,
Come, I will take you down underneath this impassive
     exterior, I will tell you what to say of me,
Publish my name and hang up my picture as that of the
     tenderest lover,
The friend the lover's portrait, of whom his friend his
     lover was fondest,
Who was not proud of his songs, but of the measureless
     ocean of love within him, and freely pour'd it forth,
Who often walk'd lonesome walks thinking of his dear
     friends, his lovers,
  .   .   .   .

Whose happiest days were far away through fields, in
     woods, on hills, he and another wandering hand in
     hand, they twain apart from other men.
                    RECORDERS AGES HENCE, pp. 89-90

Whitman and Nietzsche were astute enough to see that man is unworthy of the creator's godhead until he finds it in himself to put aside creativity's

171

concomitant impulse, the impulse to destroy. Unless man wills otherwise, man's creations, not to mention himself, are doomed. Civilization cannot be saved solely by institutions, solely by the creations of the creators. It can only be saved by those strong enough to aspire to no more for themselves than for their coevals. Only love and respect for man, not fear and worship of man's inventions, can preserve life. Of such was the kingdom of Whitman:

I hear it was charged against me that I sought to destroy
    institutions,
But really I am neither for nor against institutions,
.   .   .   .   .
Only I will establish in the Mannahatta and in every city
    of these States inland and seaboard,
.   .   .   .   .
Without edifices or rules or trustees or any argument,
The institution of the dear love of comrades.
            I HEAR IT WAS CHARGED AGAINST ME, p. 94

Those that go their own gait, erect, stepping with freedom
    and command, leading not following,
Those with a never-quell'd audacity, those with sweet and
    lusty flesh clear of taint,
Those that look carelessly in the faces of Presidents and
    governors, as to say *Who are you?*
Those of earth-born passion, simple, never constrain'd,
    never obedient.
            THE PRAIRIE-GRASS DIVIDING, p. 94

Here, indeed, are Whitman's "frailest leaves," which, nonetheless, are his "strongest lasting" since they reveal no murky intent of the unconscious but the all too painfully conscious reflection that men

172

must love one another or die (*Here the Frailest Leaves of Me*, p. 95). And, in a lighter vein, reminiscent of Marlowe's dictum, and anticipatory of Nietzsche's theorizing on sublimation, Whitman writes:

Now I think there is no unreturn'd love, the pay is certain
  one way or another,
(I loved a certain person ardently and my love was not
  return'd,
Yet out of that I have written these songs.)
  SOMETIMES WITH ONE I LOVE, p. 97

Commonplace the thought and experience, – true. But not quite so commonplace the conscious, unembarrassed admission of it. Of a kind with the parade of the bleeding heart, endemic to Werthers and Manfreds, yet with a difference. The typical *Weltschmerz* – coupled, however, with a philosophical resignation unknown to the intemperate passion of a Lara. Indissolubly intertwined with the unashamed confessional aspect, we discern the profounder awareness that life is sweet even in its bitterness, that love is the beginning of life and the ending of life, the be-all and end-all of existence. The thought also faintly echoes Emerson's notion of compensation and brings to mind the section, "The Dance Song," from the second part of *Zarathustra* where the philosopher describes his two great loves, the maidens, Love and Wisdom, and declares for the former. Perhaps Nietzsche's personal experience was not as shattering as biographers Schyberg and Asselineau assure us Whitman's was. Nevertheless, he, too, knew the bittersweet

173

truth that to live was to love and to love was to lose:

> There is bitterness in the cup of even the best love: thus it arouses longing for the Superman, thus it arouses thirst in you, the creator!

> From the heart of me I love only Life – and in truth, I love her most of all when I hate her!
> But that I am fond of Wisdom, and often too fond, is because she very much reminds me of Life!
> ZARATHUSTRA, Hollingdale, pp. 96; 132

Whitman and Nietzsche knew disappointment and despair not intermittently, or on one or two isolated occasions, but almost constantly. But their love of "infinite, teeming, mocking life" (*Broadway, Leaves of Grass*, p. 360) always saw them through their darkest hours and gravest doubts. At sixty-nine, despite his "wreck'd, old, poor and paralyzed" body, Whitman was still carolling "the undiminish'd faith – the groups of loving friends" (*A Carol Closing Sixty-nine, Leaves of Grass*, p. 352).

Like Whitman, Nietzsche's first demand upon would-be companions is that they be daring and predisposed to honor the master because they honor themselves. They must be able to share his gladness in the ostracism visited upon the unconventional. Likewise, they must love life beyond all reason, beyond all vestige of the simulacrum of true love – pity. They must be one with him in finding the goal and meaning of life in creation, in recognizing that only where there are graves are there resurrections, in scorning sand-grain discretion and

174

ant-swarm inanity, in remaining true to the earth. They must turn away from those herdsmen who revile the temporal and hold up for a worthy prize the eternal, perfect life. Zarathustra detests such herdsmen because they not only breed a contempt for the real life but because, by insinuating that only the weak and the suffering can attain a higher life, they, in effect, suggest that the aim of life is to afflict oneself with as much misery and pain as one can:

A light has dawned for me: I need companions, living ones. ... I need living companions who follow me because they want to follow themselves – and who want to go where I want to go. ... Zarathustra shall not be herdsman and dog to the herd! To lure many away from the herd – that is why I have come. The people and the herd shall be angry with me: the herdsmen shall call Zarathustra a robber.

I say herdsmen, but they call themselves the good and the just. I say herdsmen: but they call themselves the faithful of the true faith.

Behold the good and the just! Whom do they hate most? Him who smashes their tables of values, the breaker, the lawbreaker – but he is the creator.

Behold the faithful of all faiths! Whom do they hate the most? Him who smashes their tables of values, the break-er, the law-breaker – but he is the creator.

The creator seeks companions, not corpses or herds or believers.

The creator seeks fellow-creators, those who inscribe new values on new tables.

The creator seeks companions and fellow-harvesters: for with him everything is ripe for harvesting. ...

The creator seeks companions and such as know how to whet their sickles. They will be called destroyers and

175

despisers of good and evil. But they are harvesters and rejoicers. ... I will make company with creators, with harvesters, with rejoicers: I will show them the rainbow and the stairway to the Superman.

ZARATHUSTRA, Hollingdale, pp. 51-52

Nietzsche interpreted salvation by faith to mean that the heart alone, not knowledge, could bring man happiness. Similarly, to Nietzsche, the incarnation of God signified that man should not seek his salvation in infinity but should found his heaven on earth. It was not Zarathustra's way to teach his followers a reassuring faith or meticulously chart their course; like Whitman, he preferred to hurl the novice into the brine and abandon him to his own devices. For the Superman, Nietzsche wished the sapient, candid self-searching that would drive him into a cul-de-sac out of which he would be able to emerge only by finding a means of affirming life without negating this world, the world which for man is the only real one.

Nietzsche's thoughts on friendship may be understood in terms of his doctrine of self-perfection. In a paradox hardly original, he tells us our best friends may actually be found in the ranks of our worst enemies. And, somewhat more originally, he argues that, if you seek a friend, you must be prepared to fight in his behalf; and, in order to be able to fight, you must be capable of becoming a formidable adversary, a pestering gadfly. Friendship must not preclude obeying or commanding. Friendship is counterfeit and futile if you become enslaved by the one whom you befriend. Nor is

176

friendship fruitful when you choose for a friend someone who is unsure of himself, someone who lacks conviction, someone who requires of you mainly pity. The true friend is he who faithfully mirrors you to yourself. He whose masquerade of friendship is just that – a transparent disguise for parasitism – does not deserve your consideration. Would the sun be happy without those for whom it shines? And, conversely, where would man be, if anywhere, without the sun? Friendship should be altruistic: giving should afford more joy than receiving. Nietzsche believed, as Whitman did, that friendship was to play a crucial role in evolving Superman. For both, friendship was a means of challenging oneself to renewed and more vigorous effort in realizing the new dawn:

Alas, for all hermits there are too many depths. That is why they long so much for a friend and for his heights.

.   .   .   .

In your friend you should possess your best enemy. Your heart should feel closest to him when you oppose him.

.   .   .   .

You cannot adorn yourself too well for your friend: for you should be to him an arrow and a longing for the Superman. Have you ever watched your friend asleep – to discover what he looked like? Yet your friend's face is something else beside. It is your own face, in a rough and imperfect mirror.

ZARATHUSTRA, Hollingdale, pp. 82-83

Because one's neighbor is not always one's equal, and, consequently, is more likely to call forth pity instead of a desire to emulate and surpass, Zarathustra teaches not "the neighbour but the friend"

177

(*Zarathustra*, Hollingdale, p. 87). Because love of one's neighbor is an abortive if not invidious escape from hatred of oneself, Zarathustra will befriend only those who are "free from the happiness of serfs, redeemed from gods and worship, fearless and fearful, great and solitary" (*Zarathustra*, Hollingdale, p. 127). Only those who have become summer entirely and summer-noonday merit the honor of being companions to Zarathustra:

Are you a slave? If so, you cannot be a friend. Are you a tyrant? If so, you cannot have friends.
In woman, a slave and a tyrant have all too long been concealed. For that reason, woman is not yet capable of friendship: she knows only love.

.   .   .   .

'You should always be the first and outrival all others: your jealous soul should love no one, except your friend' – this precept made the soul of a Greek tremble: in following it he followed his path to greatness.

ZARATHUSTRA, Hollingdale, pp. 83; 85

The friend must not conceal one who puts his faith in others only because of an incapacity to have faith in himself. Man must not think to lose or find himself in the friend. Solitude is only a prison to those who do not love themselves sufficiently. In the first place, the friend should be a diligent pupil of Zarathustra's teachings; in the second place, he should be desirous of surpassing his master instead of using him as a crutch; and, in the third place, he should approach one step closer to the ideal envisioned by his master, to the ideal of the man who has overcome himself, to the ideal of the Superman. In the companion-pupil (friend-disciple), Nietzsche

178

sought either the potential for the superhuman or, at the least, the aspiration to contribute to the evolvement of the superhuman. In *Zarathustra*, comrade-catechumen and Superman are closely identified for several reasons: Nietzsche adduces Zarathustra as Superman; Nietzsche intends Zarathustra's teachings to point out the road to the superhuman; and Nietzsche wishes to imply only a Zarathustra, or a reasonable facsimile thereof, is deserving of his company and instruction. Nietzsche's search for the friend and quest for the Superman frequently reduces to Nietzsche's search for Nietzsche or Nietzsche's quest for Nietzsche's *Doppelgänger*. Nietzsche, like Whitman, recalls Narcissus.

In an oft-quoted letter to his sister in 1886, Nietzsche wrote that a man of spiritual depth craves friends unless he still has God as a friend, but that he (Nietzsche) had neither God nor friends. It, therefore, appears that Nietzsche demanded much more from the friend than did Socrates; in the friend, in the future Overlords of the Earth, in himself, Nietzsche frantically tried to find a succedaneum for the God-Man he deemed dead. The melancholy spectacle, the disintegration of traditional religious belief, led Arnold to *Dover Beach* and *Sweetness and Light;* it led Nietzsche to the Man-God. Yet, no matter how often he susurrated to himself the incantation – 'The world is myself. Life is myself. God is in me or else is not at all.' – he could neither realize the glow of reassurance his lucid disbelief had seemed to promise, nor exorcize the misgivings evoked by his recall of Luther's words that one genuflects before God or an idol. Somewhat like Whitman who, though he believed in the divinity of Self, found it necessary to believe in the divinity of God as well before he could be perfectly at peace with himself, Nietzsche learned that the usurpation of God's Throne by Man's Ego left something to be desired. Notwithstanding, Nietzsche remained as true (if not truer) to his love, the Superman, than did Arnold to his love in *Dover Beach*. Nietzsche was no weathercock ready to capitulate with whimpers before life's nihility.

There are mystical elements in Whitman and Nietzsche, but neither was a mystic and both were largely existential in their attitudes towards death and in their insistence on selfness as opposed to selflessness. As has been adumbrated, both viewed a stoic indifference to death as cowardice rather than courage, as a form of escape from reality, as a refusal to confront life. They told man to go through life constantly aware of the prospect of his certain death, constantly wary lest his death on the morrow render his life meaningless. They explained that, by boldly and intrepidly facing the inevitability of the final and ultimate nothingness, man conquers time and death; and that, by concentrating on what is subject to time and death, man makes of death a constitutive part of life. Whitman and Nietzsche did not conceal from themselves either the reality or the horror of death, which they found not only at the end of life but also in life's midst (in the form of sleep, sickness, and suffering).

180

They would have found it impossible to say with St. Teresa *"Muero porque no muero"* (I am dying because I cannot die). For them, life was the elimination of what was dead. They cherished the individual above all else and placed a greater emphasis on the "I" than on the "It."

But, whereas Whitman was inclined to stop with man, Nietzsche would not hear of any such thing. He argued that man is not an end in himself; that man is a bridge to an end higher than himself. However, before man can attain that higher end he must relearn how to despise himself. (The Superman, once bred, would, in turn, be replaced by another who, by adhering to his own good and evil, would repudiate his predecessor's and, at the same time, prepare the way for his own eventual disappearance and supersedure.) Man must acknowledge, that is, his shortcomings; and, once having acknowledged them, he must overcome them, and must never thereafter suffer their resurgence. He must pursue perfection (the perfection defined by his own standards) and, towards that end, must not hesitate to demolish whatever blocks his path. Nietzsche held that the basic principle of life was the unceasing evolutionary process whereby life perpetually sought to surpass itself, to elevate itself from the level it occupied at any particular time to a higher level, to reject the goal recently achieved as vain and set its sights on a more distant goal, not necessarily a higher goal but at least a different goal, perhaps even a contrary goal:

181

I teach you the friend in whom the world stands complete, a vessel of the good – the creative friend, who always has a complete world to bestow.

And as the world once dispersed for him, so it comes back to him again, as the evolution of good through evil, as the evolution of design from chance.

May the future and the most distant be the principle of your today: in your friend you should love the Superman as your principle.

ZARATHUSTRA, Hollingdale, p. 88

At the same time, Zarathustra, in one of many climactic valedictories, tells those who wish to serve under his aegis, those who aspire to be creators (that is, men whose values are of their own making and not the illusions of listless conformity, men whose reach exceeds their grasp, men whose goal never fails their aspiration) that the road they will be required to take afoot with their vision will be treacherous and infested with homicidal renegades and pistareen officialdom. As pedestrians on this road, they will experience the solitude which is "Zero at the Bone." They will know gethsemane. They will be strangers in another country, astronauts hurtling through the visible darkness and icy stillness of space, wandering exiles around whose collective neck an albatross, the deadweight of sole responsibility, will hang heavy. They must forearm themselves against the suicidal nihilism of Dostoievski's Stavrogin and against the despairing futilitarianism issuing from a sense of life's purposelessness. Above all, they must constantly be on guard lest, out of pity for man or out of their craving for companionship, they be seduced to

their own destruction by conceding society's illusory authority and authoritarian illusions:

It is terrible to be alone with the judge and avenger of
one's own law. It is to be like a star thrown forth into
empty space and into the icy breath of solitude. ...

.   .   .   .   .

... One day solitude will make you weary. ... One day
you will cry: 'I am alone!' ...

.   .   .   .   .

... One day you will cry: 'Everything is false!'

Be on your guard, too, against holy simplicity! Everything which is not simple is unholy to it: and it too, likes to
play with fire – in this case, the fire of the stake.
And be on your guard, too, against the assaults your love
makes upon you! The solitary extends his hand too
quickly to anyone he meets.
To many men, you ought not to give your hand, but only
your paw: and I should like it if your paw had claws, too.

.   .   .   .

You must be ready to burn yourself in your own flame:
how could you become new, if you had not first become
ashes?

.   .   .

Go apart and be alone with my tears, my brothers. I love
him who wants to create beyond himself, and thus perishes.
ZARATHUSTRA, Hollingdale, pp. 89-91

Patently, therefore, friend meant considerably more
to Whitman and Nietzsche than is generally understood by *amicus* or φίλος. Friend meant more to
them than confidant, *alter ego*, and disciple although
it meant these relationships also. They desired
friends because they were human and yearned for
companionship and because they were idealistic
and desired to enlighten as many as they could. In
183   addition, however, they desired friends for a reason

some might designate utilitarian rather than humanistic: they prized the friend very much in the
manner Shaw prized the human male drone and
the New Woman – as precursors of the superior
men of tomorrow. Nietzsche's Overman, in any
event, is closer to Shaw's Superman than to Carlyle's
Great Man. The prefix, over-, in Overman (*Übermensch*) refers to man's overcoming (*überwunden*)
himself, to man's conquest of his craving for domina-
tion. It should not be understood as referring to
the strong man's dictatorial rule over the weak, the
gullible, and the enslaved. Nor should it be used to
designate one who considers himself above all laws
and constraints, one whose disbelief in all values
leads him not to a revaluation but to rapine and
murder. Anarchy, like tyranny, is also slavery.
Nietzsche's ideal is not a power-crazed, barbaric
brigand intent on sating his appetites rather than
transcending his animal ancestry. Nietzsche's ideal
is the man who knows freedom is responsibility.
The Nietzschean Superman is the man who by
consenting to the world's divinity consents also to
its repeated reproduction in the course of its eternal
gyrations, and hence becomes creator of it and
himself. Judge and avenger of his own law, pos-
sessor of a new type of anguish and a new type of
happiness – a joy deeper than woe – the Nietzschean
Superman is easily able to effect Shelley's alchemy:
to transform utter desolation into gustatory delight
in our polymorphic world; to extract from his
sickness unto death the strength to transcend renunciation and resignation and to conquer freedom

184

and life anew every day; to transmute the agonies and pangs of loneliness into the milk and honey of his affirmative insight.

Nietzsche did not agree with Schopenhauer that the basic drive in all human beings is the will to life. He did not think that the Darwinian struggle for survival, the biological instinct of self-preservation enjoyed the primacy in human behavior. For the will to life, he substituted the will to power. More than pity (or compassion), more than love (sex), more than life itself, Nietzsche maintained, man desires power, self-aggrandizement (and is prepared to risk and lose his life in the effort to fulfill this desire). Hence history's abundant records of Master- &-Slave civilizations, perpetually reenacting the drama of the subjugation of the weaker by the stronger and the worship of the stronger by the weaker. Hence the bloody revolutions whenever the will of the servant was found to contain the will to be master. And hence, too, the self-immolation of the strongest, for "as the lesser surrenders to the greater, that it may have delight and power over the weakest of all, so the greatest, too, surrenders and for the sake of power stakes – life" (*Zarathustra*, Hollingdale, p. 138). The Overman, however, Nietzsche explains, is the man who is not seduced by this will to power, who does not yield to its importunities, who does not identify right with might. The Overman is the man who has overcome the man in himself, who has sublimated the will to power into creative efflux. Nietzsche instances Goethe and Julius Caesar as examples. The world must either produce such men or risk perishing in an abortive effort to satisfy Bellona's insatiability. Only such men, Nietzsche averred, could forestall the nihilistic apocalypse (which threatens and will surely come to pass in the twentieth century) by instituting a new renaissance:

Watch and listen, you solitaries! From the future come winds with a stealthy flapping of wings; and good tidings go out to delicate ears.

You solitaries of today, you who have seceded from society, you shall one day be a people: from you, who have chosen out yourselves, shall a chosen people spring – and from this chosen people, the Superman.

Truly, the earth shall yet become a house of healing! And already a new odour floats about it, an odour that brings health – and a new hope!

ZARATHUSTRA, Hollingdale, pp. 102-103

Only by the rise of such men, Nietzsche believed, could the death of God prove a blessing in disguise. And, evidently, it was precisely of such men that Whitman was thinking when he wrote:

There will soon be no more priests ... A superior breed shall take their place ... the gangs of the kosmos and prophets en masse shall take their place. A new order shall arise and they shall be the priests of man, and every man shall be his own priest. The churches built under their umbrage shall be the churches of men and women. Through the divinity of themselves shall the kosmos and the new breed of poets be interpreters of men and women and of all events and things.

PREFACE, 1855, p. 425

To Whitman and Nietzsche, the friend was, conse-   186 quently, the link to the future, the sacrificial firstling who, like themselves, had to suffer immolation in order to clear the passage to India and Zoroaster, the passage to more than India and Zoroaster. They went before; the friends brought up the rear. To their John the Baptist, the friends must be the Christ. Whitman confidently waited upon the future not only to accord him the fame and acclaim he reaped in insufficient amounts while alive, but also to bring forth those stalwart youths and nubile maidens who were to fulfill the poet's American Dream. With characteristic assurance, he foretold

A new race dominating previous ones and grander far, with new contests,
New politics, new literatures and religions, new inventions and arts.

STARTING FROM PAUMANOK, p. 23

By such denizens of Whitman's American Canaan, Whitman was to be vindicated:

Poets to come! orators, singers, musicians to come!
Not to-day is to justify me and answer what I am for,
But you, a new brood, native, athletic, continental, greater than before known,
Arouse! for you must justify me.

I myself but write one or two indicative words for the future,
I but advance a moment only to wheel and hurry back in the darkness.

I am a man who, sauntering along without fully stopping, turns a casual look upon you and then averts his face,

Leaving it to you to prove and define it,
Expecting the main things from you.

POETS TO COME, p. 13

Nietzsche indulged in the same hope (or rationalization):

I go among this people and let fall many a word; but they
know neither how to take nor to keep.
They are surprised that I have not come to rail at their
lusts and vices; and truly, I have not come to warn
against pickpockets, either!

.   .   .

I am Zarathustra the Godless: where shall I find my equal?
All those who give themselves their own will and renounce
all submission, they are my equals.

.   .   .

Oh, that you understood my saying: 'Always do what you
will – but first be such as *can will!*'
'Always love your neighbors as yourselves – but first be
such as *love themselves* –
'such as love with a great love, such as love with a great
contempt!' Thus speaks Zarathustra the Godless.

.   .   .

But why do I speak where no one has *my* kind of ears?
Here it is yet an hour too early for me.
Among this people I am my own forerunner, my own
cock-crow through dark lanes.
But *their* hour is coming! And mine too is coming!
Hourly will they become smaller, poorer, more barren
– poor weeds! poor soil!
And *soon* they shall stand before me like arid grass and
steppe, and truly! weary of themselves – and longing
for *fire* rather than for water!
O blessed hour of the lightning! O mystery before noontide! One day I shall turn them into running fire and
heralds with tongues of flame –
one day they shall proclaim with tongues of flame: It is
coming, it is near, *the great noontide!*

ZARATHUSTRA, Hollingdale, pp. 190-192

188

Like Whitman, moreover, Zarathustra called for superior offspring. Zarathustra taught that one should avoid rushing into marriage recklessly lest his wedlock prove a bad lock and eventuate in adultery, or, what is worse, in the malcontent's paranoia. Pairing should be allowed before marriage to ascertain true love and genuine compatibility. When, and only when love and compatibility had been concretely demonstrated, should couples be allowed to risk the deep plunge into matrimony. For only marriage partners well-adjusted and suited to each other would be able "not merely to reproduce, but to produce something higher," i.e., the Superman (*Zarathustra*, *Portable Nietzsche*, p. 323).

Whitman and Nietzsche envisioned the way to the man of tomorrow as the conquest and reclamation of the quicksands of tradition and morality, as a titanic agon with all tergiversators of life, as a crusade against the Christian-pie-in-the-sky vulnerary adhibited as a cure-all by the vulpine afterlifers. (Nietzsche's coinage is *Hinterwelter:* those who believe in an after life; afterworldsmen.) Whitman and Nietzsche knew the would-be traveler on their widely-heralded road would need the audacity and enterprise of Odysseus as well as the strength and perseverance of Hercules. This emprise of emprises would require a strong being, an earnest and stout person capable of yoking destiny and charting his nation's course:

189   All waits or goes by default till a strong being appears;

A strong being is the proof of the race and of the ability of
    the universe,
When he or she appears materials are overaw'd,
The dispute on the soul stops,
The old customs and phrases are confronted, turn'd back,
    or laid away.

SONG OF THE BROAD-AXE, p. 139

To such strong beings, Whitman and Nietzsche
ascribed the cognomen, pioneers. Whitman mus-
ters his trailblazers to the colors with stirring martial strains; his rousing reveille melds with the roll
of the band's booming drums. Whitman is determined to rouse from lethargy those lulled into
semi-stupor by the lotus weeds of despair, diffidence, dismay, and dysphoria:

We must march my darlings, we must bear the brunt of
    danger,...
All the past we leave behind,...
Conquering, holding, daring, venturing as we go the un-
    known ways,...
O I mourn and yet exult, I am rapt with love for all,...
Raise the mighty mother mistress,
Waving high the delicate mistress, over all the starry
    mistress, (bend your heads all,)
Raise the fang'd and warlike mistress, stern, impassive,
    weapon'd mistress,
    Pioneers! O Pioneers!...
Through the battle, through defeat, moving yet and never
    stopping,
    Pioneers! O Pioneers!
O to die advancing on!
Are there some of us to droop and die? has the hour come?
Then upon the march we fittest die, soon and sure the gap
    is fill'd,...
Not for delectations sweet,

190

> Not the cushion and the slipper, not the peaceful and the
> studious,
> Not the riches safe and palling, not for us the tame en-
> joyment,
> Pioneers! O Pioneers!
> Do the feasters gluttonous feast?
> Do the corpulent sleepers sleep? have they lock'd and
> bolted doors?
> Still be ours the diet hard, and the blanket on the ground,
> Pioneers! O Pioneers!
>
> PIONEERS! O PIONEERS!, pp. 168-70

Nietzsche's exhortation is of the same kidney albeit less martial:

> *Pioneers.* – I greet all the signs indicating that a more
> manly and warlike age is commencing. ...For it has to
> prepare the way for a yet higher age, ... the age which
> will carry heroism into knowledge, and *wage war* for the
> sake of ideas and their consequences. For that end many
> brave pioneers are now needed, who, however, cannot
> originate out of nothing, – and just as little out of the sand
> and slime of present-day civilization and the culture of the
> great cities: men silent, solitary and resolute, who know
> to be content and resolute in invisible activity: men who
> with innate dispositions seek in all things that which is *to
> be overcome* in them: ... men more imperilled, more pro-
> ductive, more happy! For believe me! – the secret of
> realizing the largest productivity and the greatest en-
> joyment of existence is, to *live in danger!* Build your
> cities on the slope of Vesuvius! Send your ships into
> unexplored seas! Live in war with your equals and with
> yourselves!
>
> JOYFUL WISDOM, pp. 218-19

Most of which, it is again interesting to note, had been said by Emerson in 1839-1840:

191   I hope in these days we have heard the last of conformity

and consistency. ...Instead of the gong for dinner, let us hear a whistle from the Spartan fife. Let us never bow and apologize more. ... Let us affront and reprimand the smooth mediocrity and squalid contentment of the times. ... Every true man is a cause, a country, and an age. ... A man Caesar is born, and for ages after we have a Roman Empire. ... All history resolves itself very easily into the biography of a few stout and earnest persons. ... Let us enter into the state of war and wake Thor and Woden, courage and constancy, in our Saxon breasts. This is to be done in our smooth times by speaking the truth. ... We are afraid of truth, afraid of fortune, afraid of death, and afraid of each other. Our age yields no great and perfect persons. We want men and women who shall renovate life and our social state.

SELF-RELIANCE

In common, Whitman and Nietzsche shared a supreme and, one is tempted to say, naively-sanguine trust in an halcyon future. In one particular, however, they did differ. Whitman's projected Garden of Adonis conforms more closely to any one of several variants of the archetypal myth of paradise. Joy conspicuously pervades the utopias of Whitman and Nietzsche to the point of surfeit, but the term is understood somewhat differently by each. Whitman's joy is the joy of paradise regained, the euphoric joy of Valhalla, the transcendental, pristine, unalloyed joy that passes understanding. It is a superterrestrial joy, more poetic than real, more mystic than human, more Blakean than Nietzschean:

A reborn race appears – a perfect world, all joy!
Women and men in wisdom innocence and health – all joy!
Riotous laughing bacchanals fill'd with joy!

192

> War, sorrow, suffering gone – the rank earth purged –
> nothing but joy left!
> The ocean fill'd with joy – the atmosphere all joy!
> Joy! joy! in freedom, worship, love! joy in the ecstasy of
> life!
> Enough to merely be! enough to breathe!
> Joy! joy! all over joy!
> THE MYSTIC TRUMPETER, pp. 327-28

In one of the few really damning contradictions in Whitman, it is joy deferred, and, therefore, at the least, a partial betrayal of the unprovisional acceptance of the human condition. Whitman's joy envisages a transfigured rather than a perfected human nature. It is the joy of the Oversoul, not of Damocles. In contrast, Nietzsche's joy is wholly mundane and derives solely from Zarathustra's service to life. No vestigial traces of Edenic nostalgia intrude upon the magnificently somber splendor of Nietzsche's rapture. Nietzsche's is the joy of Kubla Khan who, undissuaded by ancestral voices prophesying doom, took pleasure in erecting his sunny dome amid caves of ice. His is the joy of the dreamer who, although forever denied the total recall of the Abyssinian maid's song, delights in perpetually being tantalized by the prospect of such a recall. It is the joy of the youth on Keats' Grecian urn: though the youth will never consummate his passion, he is perfectly content with his lot and would not have it otherwise. It is the joy of one who has drunk the milk of the only Paradise destined for man:

193   All joy wants the eternity of all things, wants honey,

wants dregs, wants intoxicated midnight, wants graves, wants the consolation of graveside tears, wants gilded sunsets, *what* does joy not want! it is thirstier, warmer, hungrier, more fearful, more secret than all woe, it wants *itself;* it bites into *itself,* the will of the ring wrestles within it, it wants love, it wants hatred, it is superabundant, it gives, throws away, begs for someone to take it, thanks him who takes, it would like to be hated; so rich is joy that it thirsts for woe, for Hell, for hatred, for shame, for the lame, for the *world* – for it knows, oh it knows this world!

ZARATHUSTRA, Hollingdale, p. 332

Joy wants banishment in order to savor the exile's solitude and in order to hone its sword of self-reliance; joy wants torture in order to be an interpreter of human misery and in order to affirm all the elements in life's *mélange;* joy wants injustice in order to assert the innocence of life. Joy wants the eternal recurrence, which sets the seal of eternity on the world of Becoming.

Whitman's cup of joy contains dregs from the Last Judgment and several particles from the ineffable irenity of theopathy. His promised land has little to distinguish it from the topography usually associated with the state of innocence. Whitman's wish to build Jerusalem in America's green and pleasant land was sincere. But, once he had experienced the exhiliration of spiritual space flight, he evidently encountered difficulty in re-entering earth's gravitational field. To the very end, he upheld the sanctity of the senses, and, like Zarathustra, always praised laughter, dancing, and wine. Debilitating age, however, led Whitman to

194

relinquish some of Nietzsche's unnerving realism and to turn a more receptive ear to the more reassuring idealism of Emerson. A distinct shift of emphasis from body to soul is discernible. And, although body and soul continued, at least intermittently, to be one in Whitman, the soul, however imperceptibly, gained ascendancy over the body. As Wallace Stevens and other millions have pointed out: 'When one is young, everything is physical; when one is old, everything is psychic.' It is reasonable to suppose that, had Nietzsche not ceased writing at the age of forty-five, had he, instead, continued to write into a ripeold age, he might have mellowed considerably, especially in regard to his radically-obdurate naturalism. But, although human nature, according to T. S. Eliot, is able to endure only a minimal amount of reality, and, although illusion is the mode in which man exists, it is still difficult to imagine Nietzsche giving up his belief in the eternal return for the doctrine of personal immortality. Zarathustra's love songs are addressed to Life without cause, to Life without purpose, to Life forever recycling, to Life always heartrending, to Life fraught with frustration, to Life festooned with fatal fascination. Those who accuse Nietzsche of misogyny would do well to note that Zarathustra attributes to his leman almost the whole of the wardrobe of masks that set off to best advantage woman's perennial allure and infinite variety: namely, her captivating coyness, her mischievous teasing, her infuriating elusiveness, her playful prankishness, her regal aloofness, her scorn-

195

ful indifference, her perverse contrariety, her specious logic, her irresistible grace, her charming elegance, her taunting smile, her penchant for intrigue, her soulful eyes, her deceptive demureness, her melodious voice, her breathtaking beauty that redeems all her faults and follies. Of further interest is the fact that Zarathustra, teacher of laughter, secures a laugh at his own expense. He good-humoredly alludes to the advice given him earlier by an old woman who warned him: "Are you visiting woman? Do not forget your whip!" (*Zarathustra*, Hollingdale, p. 93). This is generally quoted out of context, assigned to Zarathustra-Nietzsche as a serious utterance, and thus used to misrepresent the German philosopher as a notorious woman-hater and sadist. But such misconceptions are readily dispelled when one reads one of the most enthrallingly beautiful passages in *Zarathustra* – Zarathustra's tender accents to his inamorata, Life:

Into your eyes I looked recently, O life: I saw gold blinking in your night-eye; my heart stopped in delight: a golden boat I saw blinking on nocturnal waters, a golden rocking boat, sinking, drinking, and winking again. At my foot, frantic to dance, you cast a glance, a laughing, questioning, melting rocking-glance: twice only you stirred your rattle with your small hands, and my foot was already rocking with dancing frenzy.

.   .   .   .

I leaped toward you, but you fled back from my leap, and the tongue of your fleeing, flying hair licked me in its sweep. Away from you I leaped, and from your serpents' ire; and already you stood there, half turned, your eyes full of desire.

196

I fear you near, I love you far; your flight lures me, your seeking cures me: I suffer, but what would I not gladly suffer for you?
You, whose coldness fires, whose hatred seduces, whose flight binds, whose scorn inspires:
Who would not hate you, you great binder, entwiner, temptress, seeker, and finder? Who would not love you, you innocent, impatient, wind-swift, child-eyed sinner?
Whereto are you luring me now, you never-tame extreme? And now you are fleeing from me again, you sweet wildcat and ingrate! I dance after you, I follow wherever your traces linger. Where are you? Give me your hand! Or only one finger!

.　　　　　.　　　　　.　　　　　.

Your lovely little white teeth are gnashing at me; out of a curly little mane your evil eyes are flashing at me.

.　　　　　.　　　　　.　　　　　.

Alongside me now! And swift, you malicious leaping belle! Now up and over there! Alas, as I leaped I fell. Oh, see me lying there, you prankster, suing for grace. I should like to walk with you in a lovelier place.
Love's paths through silent bushes, past many-hued plants. Or there along that lake: there goldfish swim and dance. You are weary now? Over there are sunsets and sheep: when shepherds play on their flutes – is it not lovely to sleep?

.　　　　　.　　　　　.

Oh, this damned nimble, supple snake and slippery witch! Where are you? In my face two red blotches from your hand itch. I am verily weary of always being your sheepish shepherd. You witch, if *I* have so far sung to you, now you shall cry. Keeping time with my whip, you shall dance and cry! Or have I forgotten the whip? Not I!
ZARATHUSTRA, PORTABLE NIETZSCHE, pp. 336-38

This by no means exhausts the parallels that can be researched profitably. Ready at hand, are many others. Whitman and Nietzsche, for example, were exponents of freedom and warned against any state that ignored the sovereignty of the individual. As was the case with the subjects of self-expression and self-perfection, Emerson's lead was also followed here. Some of Whitman's tiresomely wordy discourses on Democracy are discursive amplifications of the germinal idea in *The American Scholar*, 1837-38:

Every thing that tends to insulate the individual, – to surround him with barriers of natural respect, so that each man shall feel the world is his, and man shall treat with man as a sovereign state with a sovereign state, – tends to true union as well as greatness.

Whitman would never have sacrificed personal liberty for Democracy or Nationalism; Nietzsche would never have placed the welfare of the State before that of the citizen. Always, in their eyes, no price was too high, no danger too great, no ransom too dear, when individualism was at the stake. In their cosmography, man was the satellite around which all other bodies described orbits. To them, the Self was inviolable; they looked upon its desecration as tantamount to slavery. Whitman's phrenological terms and neologisms (e.g., adhesiveness, camerado, libertad) reveal the high regard he had for the individual's autonomy in government or in any other collective enterprise. As a diehard vitalist, Whitman insisted the organic bond deserved

198

primary consideration. Nonetheless, his diction in conveying the concept of many in one (e.g., linkage, adherence, coherence, correspondence, adhesion, cohesion, fusion, union, connection, correlation, relation, joining, conjoining, embracing, coupling, including, solidifying, combining, gluing, congealing) is ample proof of his abiding faith in human togetherness as well as in self-determination. In fact, in one instance, bias, largely although not entirely instinctual, together with his manic as well as mantic chauvinism, led him not only to lose sight of the universal fraternity of men but also brought him close to setting the many-in-one above the one. Although he opposed slavery and was dead set against its spread into new territories, this peerless champion of human rights, whose violently explosive vocables on freedom erupted like volcanic lava, was prepared to permit the institution to continue in the South. Why? Because the Union's preservation was his prime concern; because he resented outlanders' criticism of his America; because he believed no state had the right to dictate to any other state:

> I will make a song for these States that no one State may under any circumstances be subjected to another State,
> And I will make a song that there shall be comity by day and by night between all the States, and between any two of them.
>
> STARTING FROM PAUMANOK, p. 17

Whitman was the spokesman for all the states, and, like a mother hen clucking over her brood, he was impartial. In spite of sporadic outbursts of John Brown sentiments, he remained indifferent or, at best, lukewarm toward the plight of the slaves and toward the evil of slavery. He was angry with the abolitionists for endangering the life of what he loved most. And he indicted the South more for its treason than for its slavocracy. During the Civil War, he resented those responsible for the suffering of his white brothers, and, in *Specimen Days*, he is meticulously objective in transcribing the atrocities of North as well as South. Notwithstanding, he did brand the South "Assassin!" (*By Blue Ontario's Shore*, p. 244) and he did join, albeit in a rejected poem, the ravening ravens led by Mistress Stowe:

I say man shall not hold property in man;
I say the least developed person on earth is just as
    important and sacred to himself or herself, as the
    most developed person is to himself or herself.
I say where liberty draws not the blood out of slavery,
    there slavery draws the blood out of liberty.

SAYS, p. 402

Whitman tried to be just to the negro, but his honesty betrayed him on more than one occasion. Roger Asselineau's evidence, consisting of letters, reported conversations, and notebook entries, is conclusive in establishing that Whitman harbored a distinct prejudice against negroes to the point of physical revulsion. (*The Evolution of Walt Whitman*, Harvard University Press, 1962 Volume II, pp. 179-91). Significantly, however, not a trace of this can be detected in his verse though many, including Roger Asselineau, remark on the absence of any

effusive lyric on the Emancipation Proclamation.
In *Song of Myself*, Whitman befriends the runaway
slave and praises the splendid physique of the
negro driving a four-horse wagon (*Song of Myself*,
pp. 33-34). And, in *By Blue Ontario's Shore*, even
though he identifies them with the bondservants
and the miserable ones of all countries and of all
ages, he does espouse the cause of those exploited
by the Plantation South:

> For the great Idea, the idea of perfect and free individuals,
> For that, the bard walks in advance, leader of leaders,
> The attitude of him cheers up slaves and horrifies foreign
> despots.
> Without extinction is Liberty, without retrograde is
> Equality,
> They live in the feelings of young men and the best women,
> (Not for nothing have the indomitable heads of the earth
> been always ready to fall for Liberty.)
>
> BY BLUE ONTARIO'S SHORE, p. 246

It may be that, like Carlyle, Whitman would not
have fancied Queequeg as a bedfellow, but neither
his bias nor his obsession with his beloved Union,
made him forget that governments which enforced
obedience and allegiance by coercion rested on precarious foundations:

> To hold men together by paper and seal or by compulsion
> is no account,
> That only holds men together which aggregates all in a
> living principle, as the hold of the limbs of the body
> or the fibres of plants.
>
> BY BLUE ONTARIO'S SHORE, p. 245

201   Whitman was every word as belligerent as Thoreau

in exposing the pretensions of the State in which
majority rule could suborn minority opinion:

> I swear nothing is good to me now that ignores individuals,
> The American compact is altogether with individuals,
> The only government is that which makes minute of
>   individuals.
>
> BY BLUE ONTARIO'S SHORE, p. 249

Elsewhere, in a rejected poem, *Poem of Remem-
brance for a Girl or a Boy of these States*, he
cautioned:

> Remember, government is to subserve individuals,
> Not any, not the President, is to have one jot more than
>   you or me,
> Not any habitan of America is to have one jot less than
>   you or me.
>
> p. 393

Against tyrants, he unleashed his heaviest and most
devastating artillery:

> The menacing arrogant one that strode and advanced
>   with his senseless scorn, bearing the murderous knife,
> The wide-swelling one, the braggart that would yesterday
>   do so much,
> To-day a carrion dead and damn'd, the despised of all the
>   earth,
> An offal rank, to the dunghill maggots spurn'd.
>
> BY BLUE ONTARIO'S SHORE, p. 244

Yet, at times, as one might guess, when aglow with
his reading of Hegel, Whitman deified the omnipotent state and saw it as protector-promoter of
art, religion, and philosophy. In his less sibylline
moments, he even contemplated a utopian com-

202

monwealth managed *without* the supervision of poetic legislators. At such times, caution and conservatism made him stress law, order, and obedience instead of liberty, revolt, and individualism:

And a song make I of the One form'd out of all,
The fang'd and glittering One whose head is over all,
Resolute warlike One including and over all,
(However high the head of any else that head is over all.)
STARTING FROM PAUMANOK, p. 17

Whitman knew very well that the One manufactured out of the Many had to have sovereign dominion over the many if it were to be meaningful and operational. But his proclivity for chasing golden caches at the end of rainbows led him to the final paradoxical position we have mentioned before. With encroaching age, he saw with increasing lucidity and with some dismay, both the limitations of absolute individualism and the pitfalls of democracy. His conclusion is not so much a compromise or a strategic withdrawal from an untenable position as it is a *petitio principii*, the calm, confident prediction of a miracle that never could be brought to pass:

I have allow'd the stress of my poems from beginning to end to bear upon American individuality and assist it – not only because that is a great lesson in Nature, amid all her generalizing laws, but as counterpoise to the leveling tendencies of Democracy – and for other reasons. Defiant of ostensible literary and other conventions, I avowedly chant "the great pride of man in himself," and permit it to be more or less a *motif* of nearly all my verse. I think this

203

pride indispensable to an American. I think it not inconsistent with obedience, humility, deference, and self-questioning. Democracy has been so retarded and jeopardized by powerful personalities, that its first instincts are fain to clip, conform, bring in stragglers, and reduce everything to a dead level. While the ambitious thought of my song is to help the forming of a great aggregate Nation, it is, perhaps, altogether through the forming of myriads of fully develop'd and enclosing individuals. Welcome as are equality's and fraternity's doctrines and popular education, a certain liability accompanies them all, as we see. That primal and interior something in man, in his soul's abysms, coloring all, and, by exceptional fruitions, giving the last majesty to him – something continually touch'd upon and attain'd by the old poems and ballads of feudalism, and often the principal foundation of them – modern science and democracy appear to be endangering, perhaps eliminating. But that forms an appearance only; the reality is quite different. The new influences, upon the whole, are surely preparing the way for grander individualities than ever. To-day and here personal force is behind everything, just the same.

A BACKWARD GLANCE p. 451-52

In contrast, Nietzsche was never of two minds concerning the state. Despite his youthful patriotism, Nietzsche soon reached the conclusion that the state was the bugbear of bugbears. He pointed out that, by its very *raison d'être*, it was inimical to artistic and philosophic pursuits. He claimed that the best brains could not function to best advantage under state control; he noted that every philosopher of any talent in his own day had found it necessary to leave a state-controlled university post or had been dismissed for not truckling to moral or political prescriptives. The state was, therefore, the supreme Philistine (in Matthew Arnold's sense of the word) capable of temporary liaisons with Gretchen and Helen – humanity and art – but inevitably inclined to return to the Whore of Babylon – orientative illusions. All governments are creations of man, not vice versa. Take creation out of the hands of the individual and place it in the hands of a political abstraction, and man is enslaved. Subordinate man to the state, and you deprive him of the power of passion, doubt, happiness, and imaginative invention. Even though it has no meritorious claim or right to the office, the state aspires to what by all life's laws is man's alone. The state blocks man's path to self-fulfillment; it does not permit man to become what he is. The state is a mighty maze without a plan, a monster of such frightful mien that to see is to hate. Nietzsche contemptuously refers to it as an idol because it exacts from man the worship and tribute to which only the products of man's self-realization are entitled. With colossal effrontery, the state seizes the throne God's death left empty and proclaims far and wide that henceforth all must salaam to it; it decrees death for those who balk at doing its bidding. Like Christianity (Nietzsche, incidentally, foretold the antagonisms which would arise between Christianity and Social States) with which it coexists in collusion or which it replaces, the State defers absolute justice and thereby sanctions wholesale injustice. Wherever its influence is felt, it undermines and demoralizes. It dehumanizes man by making him an easily-replaceable cog in a

205

machine, deprives him of idenity by imposing on him a conformist uniformity, and reduces him to an animal by placing him in a purely Darwinian environment. It is an opportunist whose primary consideration is its own self-aggrandizement. It is adept in debasing coinage and secularizing ideals. Worst of all it is nihilistic by being unrealistic; its rules and prohibitions are no more mindful of things as they are than are the Church's precepts:

The state is the coldest of all cold monsters. Coldly it lies, too; and this lie creeps from its mouth: 'I, the state, am the people.'
It is a lie! It was creators who created peoples and hung a faith and a lover over them: thus they served life.

.   .   .   .

'There is nothing greater on earth than I, the regulating finger of God' – thus the monster bellows. And not only the long-eared and short-sighted sink to their knees!

.   .   .   .

It will give *you* everything if *you* worship it, this new idol: thus it buys for itself the lustre of your virtues and the glance of your proud eyes.

.   .   .   .

Just look at these superfluous people! They acquire wealth and make themselves poorer with it. They desire power and especially the lever of power, plenty of money – these impotent people!
See them clamber, these nimble apes! They clamber over one another and so scuffle into the mud and the abyss. They all strive towards the throne: it is a madness they have – as if happiness sat upon the throne! Often filth sits upon the throne – and often the throne upon filth, too.

.   .   .   .

Only there, where the state ceases, does the man who is not superfluous begin: does the song of the necessary man, the unique and irreplaceable melody, begin.

206

> There, where the state *ceases* – look there, my brothers.
> Do you not see it: the rainbow and the bridges to the
> Superman?
>
> ZARATHUSTRA, Hollingdale, pp. 75-78

Since the state is an impediment in the path of the
Superman, Nietzsche hates it. But equally if not
more hateful are those whom Zarathustra terms
poisonous tarantulas:

> I do not wish to be confused with these preachers of
> equality, nor taken for one of them. For justice speaks
> thus *to me:* 'Men are not equal.'
> And they should not become so, either! For what were my
> love of the Superman if I spoke otherwise?
> They should press on to the future across a thousand
> bridges and gangways, and there should be more and
> more war and inequality among them. ...
> Good and evil, and rich and poor, and noble and mean, ...
> they should be weapons and ringing symbols that life must
> be overcome again and again!
> Life wants to raise itself on high with pillars and steps;
> it wants to gaze into the far distance and out upon joyful
> splendour – *that* is why it needs height!
> And because it needs height, it needs steps and conflict
> between steps and those who climb them! Life wants to
> climb and in climbing overcome itself!
>
> ZARATHUSTRA, Hollingdale, pp. 124-25

It is ironic that one hailed as the *ne plus ultra*
Knight of Democracy should be found guilty of
racial bias whereas one often denounced as a
Germanic Macchiavelli and identified with Nazi
Jew-baiting should be found innocent of any ethnic
prejudice. In Whitman's behalf, it must be repeated that he took especial pains to uphold the negro's
cause in his poetry which, after all, was the only

207

legacy he intended for general public scrutiny. Milton perhaps did not, but Virgil, in the *Aeneid*, certainly omitted many personal reflections that would have defeated his purpose of glorifying Augustan Rome. Whitman believed his duty to be that of inspiring confidence and exalting his country. Intimate, spontaneous, and unconventional as his verse may appear and as the poet tells us many times it is, we know very well that Whitman labored over it with Wordsworthian thoroughness. Whether the focal center be Whitman, the Self, Man, America, or what have you, and whether its epic pretensions are justified or not, the unalterable fact is that the author intended it should be a showpiece and a gospel and hence strove for the sublimity usually associated with such endeavors. If he himself as well as his country fell far short of what he would have ideally wished them to be, he obviously was not going to announce this to the world even though he does on rare occasions censure himself as well as his native land. In his rejected poems, in the first versions of many poems, in his letters and prose, not to mention his conversation, the most demanding critic will find ample materials indicating misgivings, qualifications, and even a furtive pessimism which once in a while peeps out. Had Whitman been less obsessed with posturing as the Great Camerado and the many-faceted Uncle Sam, he might have written (or rewritten) less like the Browning of *Rabbi Ben Ezra* and *Prospice* and more like the Browning who explored the lower depths of the soul. One

208

who conceives his sacred mission as that of ex-
pressing incomparable things incomparably well
must tread gingerly lest he fail of living up to his
advance billing. Whitman was human and therefore culpable; but he was not ignoble. His Dutch
stubbornness would never consent to withdrawing
his poems of ithyphallic ardor – though Emerson
himself were the pleader. All of which is not precisely germane to our inquiry except the often
overlooked fact that Whitman shared a larger measure of Nietzsche's distrust of equality and the herd
than one would ever guess. Whitman, too, hated
life-draining uniformity and joined Nietzsche in
lambasting Carlyle's aristocratic proclivities as well
as the Scotchman's notion of the great man.

Wars of conquest, needless to say, were repug-
nant to both Whitman and Nietzsche. Like Blake,
they endorsed wars fought in the cause of political
freedom. But first-hand experience rendered physical strife extremely distasteful to them. Nietzsche
never completely recovered either his health or his
equanimity after serving as an ambulance orderly
in the Franco-Prussian War. Physical violence he
found unendurable; his father's insanity and death
following a fall haunted him like the lightning-
blasted tree is said to have haunted Swift. Whitman both was and was not so finical. Although he
carried to his grave the American youngster's love
of soldiers, parades, flags, fifes, and drums, he never
was able to forget those terrible scenes of carnage
which he steadfastly refused to shade from his
vision and which he so faithfully transcribed in

209

Specimen Days. One of the most substantial portions of his life's work, the poems comprising *Drum-Taps*, for the most part represent his thoughts, observations, experiences, and reflections associated with the Civil War. Herein hardihood and valor are celebrated with the same romantic glow they are in Scott, Tennyson, and Kipling. What is more, Whitman's songs of arms and men are not restricted to *Drum-Taps;* they abound throughout *Leaves of Grass* and disclose a species of adolescent saber rattling without counterpart in Nietzsche who admired only the courage needed to defy the world's opinion.

Although Nietzsche, unlike Whitman, did not believe in the Soul, Immortality, and God, there are many correspondences in their views on Christ and Christianity. Both respected the teaching of Christ and directed their criticisms against the Church. Once again, taking their cue from Emerson, they argued divine direction was identical with self-direction. Their quarrel was more with Religion than with religiousness, more with Faith than with faith, more with Christianity as Morality than with Christianity as Love. Whitman urged piety, reverence, and mysticism, but he abominated wishy-washy spiritualism. He continually speaks of a new religion although, as was his way, he is never very specific. In one place, the new theology seems to consist of a strange amalgam of all religions; in another, it appears to be a replacement of the bible and priests by poetry and poets; and, in still another, it is the substitution of scientific data and

210

scientists for psalms and clerics. In fact, one reason for Whitman's enthusiastic reaction to Darwinism was his conviction that science would hasten the decease of established churches:

With Science, the Old Theology of the East, long in its dotage, begins evidently to die and disappear. But (to my mind) Science – and may be such will prove its principal service – as evidently prepares the way for One indescribably grander – Time's young but perfect offspring – the New Theology – heir of the West – lusty and loving, and wondrous beautiful.

PREFACE, 1872, p. 431

Partly because he was of Quaker ancestry, partly because he was Emerson's pupil, and partly because he was possessed of much common sense though little formal schooling, Whitman, like Byron in *Don Juan*, fleered at the multiplicity of Christian denominations. Moreover, since side by side with his idealism he espoused rationalism as well as free thought, he was an ardent defender of Thomas Paine. His doctrine of self-reliance naturally made him an enemy of all and any churches and his mysticism logically dictated that he seek spiritual guidance from within rather than from without. He welcomed Christianity's "melancholy, long, withdrawing roar," and saw in it a golden opportunity for shaping the religion of the future which would be free of superstition, fables, pessimism, and dogma:

Abstract religion, I perceive, is easily led astray, ever credulous, and is capable of devouring, remorseless like fire and flame. ... We want, for these States, ... a cheerful, religious fervor, endued with the ever-present modifications of the human emotions, friendship, benevolence, with a fair field for scientific inquiry, the right of individual judgment, and always the cooling influences of material Nature.

DEMOCRATIC VISTAS, p. 494

He was beforehand in deprecating the religion which maligns life by fanatical attrition and unbelievable *mirabilia*. Religion, Whitman preceded Nietzsche in saying, must be "sweet and unimpugnable alike to little child or great savan" (*Democratic Vistas*, p. 495). Whitman was willing to be tolerant and generous to a fault, but he was firm in teaching that man's soul "can really confront Religion when it extricates itself entirely from the churches, and not before" (*Democratic Vistas*, p. 481). Here he was repeating Emerson, as he was in calling the Poet the true Son of God and in assigning to Him the task of blending Man and Nature (*Passage to India*, p. 291). For Whitman, as for Nietzsche, creation, not prayer, was true worship. "The priest departs, the divine literatus comes," Whitman evangelized (*Democratic Vistas*, p. 457). Whitman believed in immortality and, at times, was even prepared to grant that body and soul were not one and the same:

I absolve you from all except yourself spiritual bodily,
    that is eternal, you yourself will surely escape,
The corpse you will leave will be but excrementitious.

TO ONE SHORTLY TO DIE, p. 314

Whitman shared most of Nietzsche's views on Christ. In his poem, "To Him that was Crucified,"

212

he addresses Christ as one who has been seriously misrepresented. The implications are that Christ's message emphasized precisely those things which Christianity opposes: namely, non-resistance to evil; universal toleration of all faiths; an ecclesia of the heart rather than one of brick edifices; universal brotherhood of man; acceptance of man and earth as they are; a melioration in human terms:

My spirit to yours dear brother,
Do not mind because many sounding your name do not
    understand you,
I do not sound your name, but I understand you, ...
We, enclosers of all continents, all castes, allowers of all
    theologies,
Compassionaters, perceivers, rapport of men.
We walk silent among disputes and assertions, but reject
    not the disputers nor any thing that is asserted,
We hear the bawling and din, we are reach'd at by di-
    visions, jealousies, recriminations on every side,
They close peremptorily upon us to surround us, my
    comrade,
Yet we walk unheld, free, the whole earth over, journeying
    up and down till we make our ineffaceable mark
    upon time and the diverse eras,
Till we saturate time and eras, that the men and women
    of races, ages to come, may prove brethren and lovers
    as we are.
                    TO HIM THAT WAS CRUCIFIED, pp. 271-72

Nietzsche did as countless others; he read his own thinking into Christ. Like Tolstoy, he interpreted the Gospels as preachments against all violence, and as injunctions to construct the kingdom of heaven with human hands out of the earth's ma-213   terials. According to Nietzsche, Christ taught:

first, that man should consent to the world and the suffering this entailed; second, that man should not abet evil, but should seek to alleviate the sum total of misery; third, that man should not listen to the reward- &-punishment salesmen but should accept his fate joyously; fourth, that man should resist injustice not by a revengeful *sic semper* but by a passive yet firm *non serviam*. Nietzsche's Christ taught man should help man by deeds, not promises; by actions, not prayer; by eupeptic bread here, not eucharistic cake hereafter. Emerson's argument that man needed no guide, not even in the person of Christ since Christ was in every man, served Nietzsche well. He argued analogously that man as the creator of values permits the abrogation of his creativity at his own peril. He found the Church as culpable as the State in foisting upon man a pernicious morality. The Church taught man to pray that he might die; Nietzsche taught man to destroy the Church that he might live: "Every Church is a stone rolled onto the tomb of the mangod; it tries to prevent the resurrection, by force" (Quoted by Camus, *op. cit.*, p. 69). Elsewhere, in an hyperbole destined to be misread, he cried: "Rather Cesare Borgia than Parsifal" (Camus, *op. cit.*, p. 75). He appropriated the epithet, godless, and anticipated Lenin in calling Christianity and alcohol Europe's narcotics, but he did not attack Jesus. He even granted that, had Jesus lived, he might have found and crossed the bridge to Overman; he might "have learned to live and to love the earth – and laughter too" (*Zarathustra*, p. 185). Nor is this

214

all. Nietzsche was prepared to go further. He also anticipated Freud's concession to human frailty:

Only Christian *practice*, a life such as he *lived* who died on the cross, is Christian.
Such a life is still possible today, for certain people even necessary: genuine, original Christianity will be possible at all times.

THE ANTICHRIST, PORTABLE NIETZSCHE, pp. 612-13

Together with a host of others, such as Matthew Arnold, their near contemporary, and T. S. Eliot, an heir they disowned before his birth, Whitman and Nietzsche diagnosed the world's sickness as a loss of belief – not only in God, but in man and in life as well. They watched man irresistibly sucked into the Spenglerian maelstrom, engulfed by waves of despair, pitiably thrashing in nihilism's waters, scarcely hoping for rescue, actually almost welcoming the death by water so conveniently at hand. And they were determined to save his life. They felt sorry for him but they were also impatient with the folly which had precipitated him into such a plight. Zarathustra dedicated his whole life to this task, and Whitman wrote:

I seize the descending man and raise him with resistless will,
O despairer, here is my neck,
By God, you shall not go down! hang your whole weight upon me!

SONG OF MYSELF, p. 57

Only that day dawns to which man is awake. Only that endures to which man consents. Only that is

215

attainable which man wills. Only if man believes in himself is Rilke's *Zustimmung zum Da-sein* possible.

But Whitman and Nietzsche were also realists and well tutored in man's basic frailties. In the last analysis, they realized, man must save himself all by himself. And, naturally, before he can commence on this task of salvation, he must face the truth about himself:

Never was there, perhaps, more hollowness at heart than at present. ... Genuine belief seems to have left us. ... Nor is humanity itself believed in. ... We live in an atmosphere of hypocrisy throughout. ... A scornful superciliousness rules in literature. ... A lot of churches, sects, etc., the most dismal phantasms I know, usurp the name of religion. Conversation is a mass of badinage. ... In fashionable life, flippancy, tepid amours, weak infidelism, small aims, or no aims at all, only to kill time. ... The best class we show, is but a mob of fashionably dress'd speculators and vulgarians.

DEMOCRATIC VISTAS, p. 461

In a phillippic in the same vein, Nietzsche uses imagery suggestive of Eliot's hollow men and the waste land. He harps on the sterility of his contemporaries, derides their hypocrisy, laments their loss of *virtu* and creativity, likens them to scarecrows and walking-dead, denounces their defeatism, and decries their lack of confidence:

Truly, you could wear no better masks than your own faces, you men of the present! ...
And if one tests your virility, one finds only sterility! You seem to be baked from colours and scraps of paper glued together. ...

216

> All customs and all beliefs speak motely out of your
> gestures.
> He who tore away from you your veils and wraps and
> paint and gestures would have just enough left over
> to frighten the birds. ...
> I would rather be a day-labourer in the underworld and
> among the shades of the bygone! – Even the in-
> habitants of the underworld are fatter and fuller
> than you! ...
> You are walking refutations of belief itself and the fracture
> of all thought. ...
> You are unfruitful: *therefore* you lack belief. But he who
> had to create always had his prophetic dreams and
> star-auguries – and he believed in belief!
> You are half-open doors at which grave-diggers wait. And
> this is *your* reality: 'Everything is worthy of perish-
> ing.'
>
> ZARATHUSTRA, Hollingdale, pp. 142-43

Whitman and Nietzsche agreed that to help humanity emerge from the slough of despair and from
the prickly aridity of cactus land what was needed
was a creative man who not only possessed creative
ability himself but would be able to stimulate the
innate creativity of others. They were convinced
the only ruler worthy of the title was the creator.
It was their way of censuring a society too pre-
ponderantly productive and too insufficiently creative. When the product assumes more importance
as we have since been told *ad nauseam*, than the
human labor expended in making the product, the
era of the autocratic, inhuman machine commences.
Man's status as a creator is lost or minimized
drastically. The mechanical erects a barrier be-
217   tween man and his production. He is no longer a

maker; he is the manipulator of a machine. His work is subordinated to production; and he himself is subordinated to the machine. Whitman sternly insists man must not abdicate the responsibility and dignity of creation. Man must never forget he is the center from which all emanates; whatever exists exists because man exists and because man wills it to exist:

List close my scholars dear,
Doctrines, politics and civilizations exurge from you,
Sculpture and monuments and any thing inscribed any-
    where are tallied in you,
The gist of histories and statistics as far as the records
    reach is in you this hour, and myths and tales the
    same,
If you were not breathing and walking here, where would
    they all be?
The most renown'd poems would be ashes, orations and
    plays would be vacuums.

A SONG FOR OCCUPATIONS, p. 158

Nietzsche subscribed to the identical sentiments: "Instead of the judge and the oppressor, the creator," was his formula for government (Quoted by Camus, *op. cit.*, p. 273). Every act of creation, by its mere existence, denies the world of master and slave. The perfect tribute to Walt Whitman is contained in what conceivably might also be a self-portrait of Nietzsche. In it, Nietzsche recites the grounds upon which he bases his praise of the creativity and creations of the poet:

I see here a poet, who, like so many men, exercises a higher charm by his imperfections than by all that is

218

rounded off and takes perfect shape under his hands, – indeed, he derives his advantage and reputation far more from his actual limitations than from his abundant powers. His work never expresses altogether what he would really like to express, what he *would like to have seen:* he appears to have had the foretaste of a vision and never the vision itself: – but an extraordinary longing for this vision has remained in his soul; and from this he derives his equally extraordinary eloquence of longing and craving. With this he raises those who listen to him above his work and above all "works," and gives them wings to rise higher than hearers have ever risen before, thus making them poets and seers themselves; they then show an admiration for their originator of their happiness, as if he had led them immediately to the vision of his holiest and ultimate verities, as if he had reached his goal, and had actually *seen* and communicated his vision. It is to the advantage of his reputation that he has not really arrived at his goal.

JOYFUL WISDOM, pp. 110-11

Such is the vision we have been examining: the vision which counsels the conquest not the circumvention of Circe; the vision which perceives one is pregnant only with one's own child; the vision which mediates between the man against the sky and the hardly discernible star-splinter; the vision which recognizes the world-weary as cowards and the depreciators of life as etherized patients; the vision which rejoices in the conditions of life as they actually are. Sartre describes our human lot as a stark quest after that which can never be realized in itself or in its finite surrogate. Whitman and Nietzsche advised just the opposite. They taught us to respond to any and every occurrence in life with the reaction: 'Was *that* life? Well then! Once more!' They taught us to think for ourselves, to approach opposing authorities with caution and, at the same time, to investigate such authorities without preconceptions and without specific ends in view.

BIBLIOGRAPHY

WALT WHITMAN

Allen, Gay Wilson. THE SOLITARY SINGER: A CRITICAL BIOGRAPHY OF WALT WHITMAN. New York: The Macmillan Company, 1955.

Allen, Gay Wilson. LEAVES OF GRASS. Signet CT23. With an introduction by. New York: The New American Library, 1955.

Asselineau, Roger. THE EVOLUTION OF WALT WHITMAN, Volume II: The Creation of A Book. Cambridge: Harvard University Press, 1962.

Miller, James E., JR. A CRITICAL GUIDE TO LEAVES OF GRASS. Chicago: Chicago University Press, 1957.

Schyberg, Frederik. WALT WHITMAN. Translated from the Danish by Evie Allison Allen with an introduction by Gay Wilson Allen. New York: Columbia University Press, 1951.

FRIEDRICH NIETZSCHE

Aiken, Henry D. THE AGE OF IDEOLOGY. Mentor MD 185. Selected with introduction and commentary by. New York: The New American Library, 1956.

Blackham, H. J. SIX EXISTENTIALIST THINKERS. Harper Torchbook TB1002. New York: Harper & Brothers, 1959.

Desan, Wilfrid. THE TRAGIC FINALE: AN ESSAY ON THE PHILOSOPHY OF JEAN-PAUL SARTRE. Harper Torchbook TB1030. New York: Harper & Brothers, 1960.

Eliade, Mircea. COSMOS AND HISTORY: THE MYTH OF THE ETERNAL RETURN. Harper Torchbook TB50. New York: Harper & Brothers, 1959.

Gaultier, Jules de. FROM KANT TO NIETZSCHE.

Translated by Gerald M. Spring. The Wisdom Library. New York, 1961.

Heinemann, F. H. EXISTENTIALISM AND THE MODERN PREDICAMENT. Harper Torchbook TB28. New York: Harper & Brothers, 1958.

Kaufmann, Walter. NIETZSCHE: PHILOSOPHER, PSYCHOLOGIST, ANTICHRIST. New York: Meridian Press, 1956.

INDEX

223

229

UNIVERSITY OF NORTH CAROLINA
STUDIES IN THE GERMANIC LANGUAGES
AND LITERATURES

Publication Committee

FREDERIC E. COENEN, EDITOR

WERNER P. FRIEDERICH GEORGE S. LANE

JOHN G. KUNSTMANN HERBERT W. REICHERT

1. Herbert W. Reichert. THE BASIC CONCEPTS IN THE PHILOSOPHY OF GOTTFRIED KELLER 1949. Pp. 164. Paper $ 3.00.
2. Olga Marx and Ernst Morwitz. THE WORKS OF STEFAN GEORGE. Rendered into English. 1949. Out of print.
3. Paul H. Curts. HEROD AND MARIAMNE, A Tragedy in Five Acts by Friedrich Hebbel, Translated into English Verse. 1950. Pp. 96. Cloth $ 3.00.
4. Frederic E. Coenen. FRANZ GRILLPARZER'S PORTRAITURE OF MEN. 1951. Pp. xii, 135. Cloth $ 3.50.
5. Edwin H. Zeydel and B. Q. Morgan. THE PARZIVAL OF WOLFRAM VON ESCHENBACH. Translated into English Verse, with Introductions, Notes, and Connecting Summaries. 1951, 1956, 1960. Pp. xii, 370. Paper $ 4.50.
6. James C. O'Flaherty. UNITY AND LANGUAGE: A STUDY IN THE PHILOSOPHY OF JOHANN GEORG HAMANN. 1952. Out of print.
7. Sten G. Flygt. FRIEDRICH HEBBEL'S CONCEPTION OF MOVEMENT IN THE ABSOLUTE AND IN HISTORY. 1952. Out of print.
8. Richard Kuehnemund. ARMINIUS OR THE RISE OF A NATIONAL SYMBOL. (From Hutten to Grabbe.) 1953. Pp. xxx, 122. Cloth $ 3.50.
9. Lawrence S. Thompson. WILHELM WAIBLINGER IN ITALY. 1953. Pp. ix, 105. Paper $ 3.00.
10. Frederic Hiebel. NOVALIS. GERMAN POET - EUROPEAN THINKER - CHRISTIAN MYSTIC. 1953. Pp. xii, 126. 2nd rev. ed. 1959. Paper $ 3.50.
11. Walter Silz. Realism and Reality: Studies in the German Novelle of Poetic Realism. 1954. Third printing, 1962. Pp. xiv, 168. Paper $ 4.00.
12. Percy Matenko. LUDWIG TIECK AND AMERICA. 1954. Out of print.
13. Wilhelm Dilthey. THE ESSENCE OF PHILOSOPHY. Rendered into English by Stephen A. Emery and William T. Emery. 1954, 1961. Pp. xii, 78. Paper $ 1.50.
14. Edwin H. Zeydel and B. Q. Morgan. GREGORIUS. A Medieval Oedipus Legend by Hartmann von Aue. Translated in Rhyming Couplets with Introduction and Notes. 1955. Out of print.
15. Alfred G. Steer, Jr. GOETHE'S SOCIAL PHILOSOPHY AS REVEALED IN CAMPAGNE IN FRANKREICH AND BELAGERUNG VON MAINZ, With three full-page illustrations. 1955. Pp. xiv, 178. Paper $ 4.00.
16. Edwin H. Zeydel. GOETHE THE LYRIST. 100 Poems in New Translations facing the Original Texts. With a Biographical Introduction and an Appendix on Musical Settings. 1955. Pp. xviii, 182. 2nd ed. 1958. Paper $ 1.75.
17. Hermann J. Weigand. THREE CHAPTERS ON COURTLY LOVE IN ARTHURIAN FRANCE AND GERMANY. Out of print.
18. George Fenwick Jones. WITTENWILER'S „RING" AND THE ANONYMOUS SCOTS POEM „COLKELBIE SOW". Two Comic-Didactic Works from the Fifteenth Century. Translated into English. With five illustrations. 1956. Pp. xiv, 246. Paper $ 4.50.
19. George C. Schoolfield. THE FIGURE OF THE MUSICIAN IN GERMAN LITERATURE. 1956. Out of print.
20. Edwin H. Zeydel. POEMS OF GOETHE. A Sequel to GOETHE THE LYRIST. New Translations facing the Originals. With an Introduction and a List of Musical Settings. 1957. Pp. xii, 126. Paper $ 3.25. Out of print.
21. Joseph Mileck. HERMANN HESSE AND HIS CRITICS. The Criticism and Bibliography of Half a Century. 1958. Out of print.
22. Ernest N. Kirrmann. DEATH AND THE PLOWMAN or THE BOHEMIAN PLOWMAN. A Disputatious and Consolatory Dialogue about Death from the Year 1400. Translated from the Modern German Version of Alois Bernt. 1958. Pp. xviii, 40. Paper $ 1.85.
23. Edwin H. Zeydel. RUODLIEB, THE EARLIEST COURTLY NOVEL (after 1050). Introduction, Text, Translation, Commentary, and Textual Notes. With seven illustrations. 1959, Second printing, 1963. Pp. xii, 165. Paper $ 4.50.
24. John T. Krumpelmann. THE MAIDEN OF ORLEANS. A Romantic Tragedy in Five Acts by Friedrich Schiller. Translated into English in the Verse Forms of the Original German. 1959. Out print.
25. George Fenwick Jones. HONOR IN GERMAN LITERATURE. 1959. Pp. xii, 208. Paper $ 4.50.